CLAN LINE IN PHOTOGR

Volume III
The Final Years 1945 - 1986

Compiled by Tony Blackler

an publication

Published by:- Avid Publications, Garth Boulevard
Bebington, Wirral,
Merseyside.UK
CH63 5LS
Telephone / Fax: (44) 0151 645 2047
e-mail info@avidpublications.co.uk
website http//:www.avidpublications.co.uk

Further copies of this book, and the first two volumes in the series, *The First 40 Years: 1878 - 1918*, and *From Peace to Peace - 1918 - 1945*, as well as other Avid Publications are available from the above.

CLAN LINE IN PHOTOGRAPHS - VOLUME III
THE FINAL YEARS 1945 - 1986

by TONY BLACKLER
ISBN 1 902964 0 55 © Tony Blackler 2003
A CIP record for this book is available from the British Library

Front Cover: Clan Macgillivray (see p101)
Rear Cover: Clan Macgowan (see p107)

OTHER BOOKS AND VIDEOS AVAILBLE DIRECT FROM AVID PUBLICATIONS ARE DETAILED AT THE REAR OF THIS BOOK

INTRODUCTION

At the start of World War II the Cayzers operated 68 vessels under several company names within the Cayzer Irvine Group. Sir August Cayzer died in 1943 and was succeeded by Sir Herbert Cayzer who had been knighted in 1937 and became Lord Rotherwick. After the Second World War the Cayzer family set about rebuilding the fleet again. The fleet had been reduced to 36 ships and to replace them 26 wartime standard ships were purchased. The first of a new class of post-war ships was the Clan Maclaren (II). She entered the fleet in 1946 and was soon followed by other "Mac L's". Many of the immediate post-war ships were designed to carry up to 12 passengers and they were equipped with heavy lift derricks.

In 1952 the company diversified by forming Scottish Tankers Ltd. and from then on further diversification took place with acquistions and mergers. The most notable merger took place in 1956 when British & Commonwealth Shipping Co. Ltd. (B&C) was formed on the merger of the Union- Castle Mail Steam Ship Co. Ltd. and its associated company, King Line Ltd. All the other companies including Greenock Dockyard came within the Group. Union-Castle continued to operate its services separately although personnel were largely interchangeable. B&C did not own the ships as they remained under the ownership of the various companies within the group, often being transferred internally between the companies.

In 1958 the Chairman, Lord Rotherwick, died, and his nephew, the son of the late Sir August Cayzer Bt., Sir Nicholas Cayzer Bt., took over as Chairman. The 2nd Lord Rotherwick, the grandson of the founder, Charles Cayzer, became Deputy Chairman. B&C continued to diversify by including air industries in the group. This was a time when air travel was starting to become dominant in the passenger market. The group was co-operating very closely with Safmarine and its associated company, Springbok Line. Ships were transferred between the companies, but generally not the personnel.

In 1962 Hector Whaling came into the B&C Group and the two tankers were retained under the flag of Scottish Tankers although they retained their Hector Whaling livery. The following year the seven ships of Bowater Steamship Co. Ltd. were placed under Cayzer Irvine management but remained under Bowater control but the officers and crew became integrated. As with the Union-Castle ships, they do not appear in this work as they were not strictly controlled by Clan Line operations.

In 1966 the Greenock Dockyard Co. Ltd. was taken over by Scotts and the last Clan Line ship, CLAN ALPINE (V), being built at the time was completed by Scotts. From then on world events and the advent of container ships saw the decline of Clan Line and other companies in the Cayzer Empire. Some bulk carriers and tankers were built and operated within the various companies wearing an assortment of liveries. The SCOTTISH EAGLE (II) was the last ship to leave the Cayzer Irvine fleet in 1986, having served in the Falklands during the conflict. Strictly not a Clan she was manned by B&C personnel and had two red bands on her funnel, albeit with a thin blue one in between them. She is included in this volume to bring the story to an honourable conclusion.

In 1980 the actual Clan fleet had reduced to five ships but the company now operated within the Beacon Consortium. This was a consortium of companies that chartered container ships to operate the UK - Europe - East African trade instead of conventional ships. The operation more and more came under the control of Overseas Container Lines (OCL) and the Clan and other companies' presence gradually disappeared. Some B&C personnel were appointed to help operate these chartered ships, mainly as supercargoes. Their job was to ensure smooth operations of a new service, both ashore and afloat.

Sir Nicholas Cayzer, now Lord Cayzer, was a very astute businessman and this was very much in evidence in 1987 when he sold the British & Commonwealth Group. The stock market collapsed just three days later!

Lord Rotherwick died in June 1996 aged 83. His wife had pre-deceased him in 1978 and their eldest son, Herbert Robin Cayzer, born in 1954, succeeded to the peerage. Lord Cayzer, Sir Nicholas, died in April 1999 aged 89. His wife had died in 1995 and they had two daughters. He had been created a life peer in 1982.

Effectively, with his death the last links with the once mighty Clan Line disappeared, except for the memories and friendships which remain with former employees of the Cayzer family, ashore and afloat. These three books are dedicated to those who still retain those bonds and I hope some of the contents will stir even more memories and anecdotes that can be recorded for history.

The Author comes from a long line of seafarers, going back several generations. In 1959 he went to King Edward VII Nautical College, London and joined British India as a deck cadet in January 1960. Afer gaining his second mates cert in 1963, he served on many Clan vessels. He passed Mates in 1965 and Masters in 1968, all in London. Swallowing the anchor in 1983 he joined the staff at Warsash Nautical College as a lecturer, teaching mainly seamanship and cargo work. Since 1993 as a part time lecturer. Tony's other activities include, writing monthly and other articles for *Sea Breezes* Magazine, marine photography, researching family history, and a couple of other maritime related projects.

This is his third compilation of photographs and meticulously researched information in the *'Clan Line in Photographs'* series, having completed Volume I & 2. He is a member of the Nautical Institute, the World Ship Society, The Thames Ship Society, the Paddle Steamer Preservation Society, and many other maritime organisations.

His daughter, Ann, is the latest member of the 'Blackler Clan' to take up seafaring. As this book is published she is at college preparing for her final OOW Cert. exams..

ACKNOWLEDGEMENTS

In compiling this volume of Clan Line ships I wish to acknowledge the invaluable works already in print of the following authors and publications:

Merchant Fleets in Profile (various volumes, principally No. 33) by Duncan Haws.

A Victorian Shipowner (a biography of Charles Cayzer produced for the Clan Line Centenary dinner in 1978) by Augustus Muir and Mair Davies, (published by Cayzer, Irvine & Co. Ltd.)

Lloyd's Register of Ships, many years' editions held in Southampton Central Library, Warsash Maritime Centre Library and my own volumes.

Clan Line 1878 - 1978 by T. J. Culpin. (A thesis lodged in the library of Warsash Maritime Centre, formerly the School of Navigation, Warsash, Hampshire).

Marine News, 1947 to the present, Journals of the World Ship Society, (WSS).

Sea Breezes, 1919 to the present.

Personal records, Tony Blackler.

Anon, document held in Warsash Maritime Centre Library.

Union-Castle Line, A Fleet History, Peter Newall (Carmania Press 1999).

Maritime Guide 1990, Lloyd's Register.

The Liberty Ships, 2nd Edition, L. A. Sawyer & W. H. Mitchell (Lloyd's of London Press 1985).

Idyll of the Kings, (History of King Line 1889-1979), Alan S. Mallett, (WSS 1980).

Stag Line 1817-1983, Nicholas J. Robinson, (WSS 1984).

Photographs, come mainly from my own collection. The source of photos, where known, is acknowledged on the pages containing the ships' details. My thanks go to all those people who have sent me photos to keep or to copy, whether they were used or not.

NOTES AND ABBREVIATIONS

If it had not been for the photographs taken and collected by Bob Briscoe and his idea of publishing his collection these three volumes may never have been produced. To his collection I have added my own and I then pondered over how to put them in a logical order. I eventually concluded that they should not be in the same order that many fleet histories use; that of the date upon first entering a company's service. I decided to use the chronological order of the Official Number (O.N.) assigned to the ships upon entering the British Register. As most ships were registered originally in Glasgow, this order generally allows the reader to follow the developments in ship design over a century. This chronology does not always work, as can be seen with ships acquired from abroad, bought from other companies and acquired with take-overs, such as King Line. Wartime built or managed ships may have Official Numbers issued by many other ports and may have been from an older block of numbers assigned earlier and used slower than other ports. Those first registered elsewhere are annotated against the O. N., which inevitably means that the sequence is not always true to date of build or acquisition so there is some overlap with the previous volume. As some classes of ship were built at the same time as other classes, there is some overlapping of dates, but the same rule applies in that the ship whose details are listed is in Official Number chronology. Her sisters may not be in the same order (or in the same block of numbers) if readers look the numbers up.

From 1965, ships were given a unique number by Lloyd's Register of Ships (LR number) which has since become the International Maritime Organisation (IMO) number. This number comprised six digits starting with a 5 and ran consecutively from the first ship in that year's register. In 1968 a seventh digit was added at the end. Where known I have given the seven figure number. The number is allocated when a ship is ordered to be built.

This volume is sub-titled "The Final Years 1945 - 1986" but I have taken the liberty of including some ships that were built during the war years as they were part of the post-war fleet and many people reading this volume will have fond, or not so fond, memories of them. A great number of the ships in this volume were well known and are well remembered by those of us who served in Clan Line and the other companies in the Group. In 1956 the Union-Castle Group came into Cayzer Irvines' ownership bringing into the Group the ships of the Union-Castle Mail Steam Ship Co. Ltd., and King Line Ltd. The company became known as the British & Commonwealth (B & C) Group, but all the ships remained under Cayzer Irvine management although they sailed under the various flags of the old companies. Many ships were transferred, on paper, between companies and it was often the case that those serving on the ships were not always aware of which company within the group was operating their ship and when. Sometimes the funnel colours were changed, sometimes not. Sometimes the names were changed, but even then they could revert and sail for another company. For this reason I have included in this volume ships within the group, which may or may not have actually sailed under the Clan Line house flag. The Union-Castle mail ships are not included as they remained on the mail run. I have also kept the Bowater ships out of the volume as they remained under Bowater's control, but for some years they were crewed by B & C personnel. Just as the ships were transferred between companies, so were the officers and sometimes the crews.

It was noticed at the time by staff and is apparent in the book, that many ships were "paper transferred" to King Line Ltd. just prior to their sale. It was often an indication to sea staff, that the ship on which they were serving, was about to be sold if ownership changed to King Line. They could expect visits from potential buyers after that. This was not always the case but it was fairly general.

Many of the ships of this era were photographed in colour, unlike most of those built during the time covered by the previous volumes. Readers will find that some ships are depicted in colour and others are not. There is no particular reason for this, just a matter of choosing the best photograph.

Most of the ships built during the period covered by this volume were part of a class and I have included the names of all those within the class, even if some others are included in this volume. I sailed on all three "MacG's" and as they had distinct and interesting careers, which are good examples of the varying lives of the Clan ships, all three of this class have been included. In my opinion, the Clan MacG's were the strongest and probably the best ships built for Clan Line in the later years. It was a pity that the container age overtook them and that they were not built to be converted, easily, to carry the modern box cargo. Hence their relatively short life spans.

Gross and net tonnages (grt & nrt) are those given for the ship shortly after her first survey. These figures may change considerably and frequently during the life of a ship. They indicate the volumetric size of a ship, 1 ton = 100 cubic feet of space.

In the first two volumes of this series dimensions are generally registered length (between perpendiculars), extreme breadth and moulded depth. These figures are in feet and tenths of feet. Dimensions may change over time as ship measurement rules change. After World War 2 length overall is the length usually quoted. Metric measurements came in later, but I have kept to Imperial measurements for standardisation, as most of the ships were built under that system.

The Summer draught, where given, is the amount of ship under water when she is fully loaded to the Summer loadline and the later ships are shown with the corresponding deadweight tonnage (dwt).

The engine details are given for engines as built. Over a period of years engines may be modified and re-rated in terms of power. Power terms also change over the years, as do the methods of calculation. The size of cylinders and the stroke of the pistons usually stayed the same. During this period some ship's engines were changed from coal to oil. This also affected specifications. After 1957 engine sizes were given in metric measurements and the Nominal Horse Power (NHP) was omitted from the registers. Unlike the previous volumes,

I have given the speed of the ships in knots (nautical miles per hour) as given in the registers or in other publications. Ships' speeds are only a guide as speed is influenced by many factors, often beyond the control of the ships' staff.

I have included the builders' yard numbers, where known, as I know many ship enthusiasts like to be given this number as it provides an additional identification and reference for the ship. Like the Official Number (O. N.) and the Lloyd's Register Number it is unique, but unlike the O. N. it cannot be changed. The O. N. will often change with a change of flag.

From 1964 Lloyd's Register of Shipping adopted a new numbering system with six figures known as the Lloyd's Register (LR) Number. The first number was a "5". It started in alphabetical order so it will be seen that many Clan ships are in a sequence. In 1968 a seventh figure was added at the end of the sixth. This unique number is kept for the entire life of the ship and is now known as the IMO (International Maritime Organisation) Number. Some flag states have now adopted this number as the ship's official number.

Occasionally, an item of data is not available in the usual sources and where this occurs a ? is inserted against the heading.

A potted history is given before details of the disposal of all ships. The dates and events are not fully documented here due to space restrictions. Readers may find that some stories catch their attention and some of these may be followed up in other publications; many of which are mentioned in the Bibliography, but official records, if available, may contain more detail. Sometimes details are given from my own notes made on the ships on which I served, and from former colleagues who have related incidents to me. I thank them all.

ABBREVIATIONS NOT EXPLAINED ELSEWHERE:

LP = low pressure DR = double reduction WSPL = World Ship Society Photo Library
dwt = deadweight tons   MOWT = Ministry of War Transport.
T3 = triple expansion engine followed by the cylinder diameter and piston stroke.

To Bombay - by Douglas Boyd

Both tugs are in attendance, one astern and one ahead,
And the order comes from our Clan's bridge to let go,
"She's off the berth now, Sir", and the Master nods his head,
And the Third Mate at the engine telegraph rings "Ahead Slow",
Pilot leaves at the Bar and "H" flag is pulled down,
Log streamed, and we're now full away,
Goodbye wintry Britain and cold Birkenhead town,
As we voyage,
Across the world,
To Bombay.

Cape Finisterre's light, flashing bright in the night,
The coast of Portugal slips swiftly away,
Past Rock of Gibraltar, British emblem of might,
And heading East, towards dawn of day,
The climate becomes warm, with the sky clear and bright,
And Master has decided that we change uniforms to white,
On balmy days like these, it's a delight to be,
On a fine British ship, on a cobalt blue sea.

Three lights ahead, on a reciprocal course,
"Dig out the Signal Lamp" and let's practice our Morse,
"What Ship, Where Bound?" probably a Dutchman or Greek,
But she's Bibby's "*Warwickshire*", with holds full of teak,
Five days through the Med to Egypt's Port Said,
Past Algiers, and Malta, Cape Bon,
To drop some parcels of cargo, have fresh water supplied,
And top up the bunkers before going on.

In the Great Bitter Lake, we stop and drop our port hook,
And lean on the bridge rail and have a good look,
The Northbound convoy is stirring, and, picking up speed,
B.I's splendid white "*Uganda*" is taking the lead,
With "*Floristan, Salsette, City of Brisbane, Elpenor,
Helenus , Mahronda, Martaban*" and "*Benmhor*",
A funnel we know, two red bands on black,
"*Clan MacLaren*" from Colombo, full of tea, and heading back,
What a magnificent stately procession,
The pride of Britain's fleet,
Bringing Chalna's jute for our carpets,
And Australian apples for us to eat.

We pass out of the Canal at Suez, into searingly hot Red Sea,
This is now petroleum country for, as far as you can see,
A long long line of tankers, hauling oil to the West,
Over there is Shell's three island "*Haminella*", and a smart blue-painted Maersk,
There's B.P.'s pristine "*British Kestrel*", and "*Caltex Mozambique*",
And another Shell, "*Achatina*", and an unknown rusty Greek,
All very low in the water,
Full of products or Arabian crude,
They are our European lifeline,
Carrying machinery's liquid food.

At Aden, discharge the Navy's stores into lighters,
For that big Aircraft Carrier and her fighters,
And some Destroyers and a Frigate in the bay,
Put the engines on stand-by, slip the buoys, a glorious orangey- pink-red sky,

Goodnight Arabia, full speed ahead, and now we're away,
Ship steering North East, in a strengthening breeze,
Everything well battened down, as we expect heavy seas,
Wind scoops retracted, and all ports are screwed tight,
We pitch and roll constantly, to the Indian Ocean's might.

There's Strick's colourful "*Khuzistan*", going very fast,
We pass about a mile apart, and she salutes us with a blast,
Attractive Gulf-run "*Dwarka*", far away to port,
Hain's "*Tremorvah*" and Reardon Smith's "*Welsh City*",
And a Liberian war-built Fort,
A Scindia Jala-boat crosses, much closer than a cable,
And there's no doubt in our minds what's on HER dinner table,
She's moving really quite slowly, in no particular hurry,
The following wind carries to us, a strong aroma of their curry.

Ten days to discharge our heavy cargo, railway lines, industrial parts,
Then clean the holds, consult the loading plan, correct the Navigational charts,
Evening visits to the B.I. Club, enjoy an ice-cold beer,
Talk shop in elegant surroundings, lots of news and gossip to hear,
Meet friends from "*Karanja*" and "*Kampala*", "*Clan MacInnes, Santhia*",
See "*City of Karachi*" arrive, and departure of "*Sangola*",
We're loading cloth and carpets, tea and sisal, coir mats,
Manganese for industry, fishmeal to feed the cats,
Our ship is now ready, pilot aboard, and rigged for sea,
Until next time,
"Al-vee-dah", India,
Land of spice and rice, rupee.

CLAN LINE IN PHOTOGRAPHS
VOLUME III
The Final Years 1945 - 1986

by Tony Blackler

CLAN MACDOUGALL (III)

LR Number	5075048
Official Number	169411
Signal Letters	GFBQ
GRT as built	9725
NRT	5556
Dimensions in feet	loa 505.5 x 64.7
Summer Draught	29' 6" at 9770 dwt.
Built by	Greenock Dockyard Co. Ltd.
Year	1944/5
At	Greenock
Yard Number	455
Engine type	B&W, 2 x 10 cylinders, 4 stroke, single acting, twin screws.
Speed	16
Built by	J. G. Kincaid & Co. Ltd.
At	Greenock
History	Near sister to **CLAN MACDONALD** (IV) (1939 built, see Vol. 2).

1943, November 10: launched for Clan Line Steamers Ltd.

1960: transferred to Houston Line (Cayzer Irvine & Co. Ltd.).

1971: sold to Castle Shipping Co. Ltd., Limassol, Cyprus. Renamed **VRYSI.**

Disposal

1971, December: broken up by Li Chon Steel & Iron Works at Kaohsiung, Taiwan.

Photo credit	M. Lindsay

CLAN CHISHOLM (II)

Official Number   169420

Signal Letters   GFBY

GRT as built   9581

NRT   5083

Dimensions in feet   loa 487.7 x 63.0

Summer Draught   28' 4½" at 9922 dwt.

Built by   Greenock Dockyard Co. Ltd.

Year   1944

At   Greenock

Yard Number   457

Engine type   T3 x 2, 26", 42", 68", - stroke 48" + LP turbine + DR gear to twin screws.

Speed   15

Built by   J. G. Kincaid & Sons Ltd.

At   Greenock

History   Sister to **CLAN CHATTAN (III)** and **CLAN CUMMING (III).**

1944, June 23: launched for Clan Line Steamers Ltd.

1962: transferred to King Line Ltd.

Disposal

1962, August 19: arrived Hong Kong for scrapping.

Photo credit   WSPL.

4

CLAN CUMMING (III)

Official Number	169480
Signal Letters	GFBZ
GRT as built	7812
NRT	3326
Dimensions in feet	loa 486.5 x 63.0
Summer Draught	28' 4½" at 9990 dwt.
Built by	Greenock Dockyard Co. Ltd.
Year	1946/8
At	Greenock
Yard Number	459
Engine type	T3 x 2, 26", 42", 68", - stroke 48" + a LP turbine + DR geared.
Speed	15
Built by	J. G. Kincaid & Sons Ltd.
At	Greenock
History	Sister to **CLAN CHATTAN (III)** and **CLAN CHISHOLM (III)**.

1946, May 3: launched for Clan Line Steamers Ltd.

Disposal

1962, October 18: arrived at Vigo, Spain, for scrapping.

Photo credit   D. Wittridge.

CLAN MACLAREN (II)

LR Number 5075153
Official Number 169488
Signal Letters GSSC
GRT as built 6021
NRT 3344
Dimensions in feet loa 466.0 x 60.9
Summer Draught 26' 0¾" at 8804 dwt.
Built by Greenock Dockyard Co. Ltd.
Year 1946/12
At Greenock
Yard Number 463
Engine type Doxford, 2 stroke, single acting, 6 cylinders.
Speed 15
Built by Barclay Curle & Co. Ltd.
At Glasgow
History Sister to **CLAN MACLEAN (III), CLAN MACLAY** and **CLAN MACLEOD (IV)**.
The first class built after World War 2. They were known as the "Clan MacL's". Hot water to the officer's cabins was not installed until the early 1970's!
1946, September 25: launched for Clan Line Steamers Ltd.
1959: transferred to Houston Line.
1961: reverted to Clan Line, but sometime later transferred to Hector Whaling Ltd.
1967: transferred from Hector Whaling Ltd. to Clan Line.
1976: sold to Seymour Shipping Ltd., London. Renamed **SEEMOR**.
Disposal
1977, May: arrived at Gadani Beach, Pakistan, for breaking up.
Photo credit Real Photo Co.

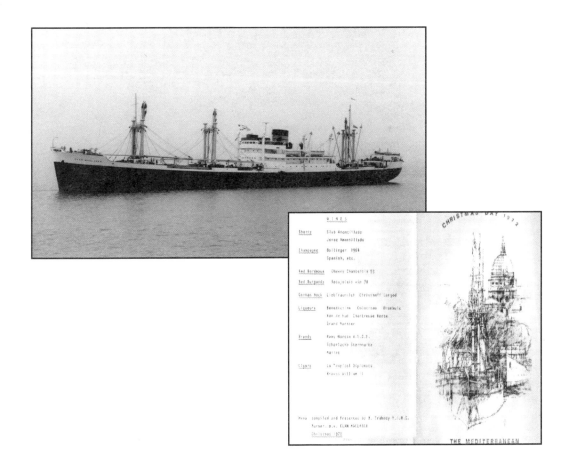

9

CLAN MACLACHLAN (II)

LR Number	5075171
Official Number	169493
Signal Letters	GSRB
GRT as built	6365
NRT	3178
Dimensions in feet	loa 466.0 x 60.8
Summer Draught	26' 0¾" at 8814 dwt.
Built by	Greenock Dockyard Co. Ltd.
Year	1947/6
At	Greenock
Yard Number	464
Engine type	Steam turbines x 3, single reduction geared.
Speed	15
Built by	D. Rowan & Co. Ltd.
At	Glasgow
History	Sister to **CLAN MACLENNAN.**

These two steam ships and the three motor ships, which were very similar, were all known by Clan Line staff as the "Clan MacL's".

1946, December 23: launched for Clan Line Steamers Ltd.

1971: transferred to King Line Ltd.

Disposal

1971, September 23: delivered to breakers at Shanghai, China, for scrapping.

Photo credit   Real Photo Co.

CLAN MACLEAN (III)

LR Number	5075177
Official Number	169500
Signal Letters	GSWX
GRT as built	6017
NRT	3328
Dimensions in feet	loa 466.0 x 60.9
Summer Draught	26' 0¾" at 8804 dwt.
Built by	Greenock Dockyard Co. Ltd.
Year	Greenock
At	1947/10
Yard Number	465
Engine type	Doxford, 2 stroke, single acting, 6 cylinders.
Speed	15
Built by	Barclay, Curle & Co. Ltd.
At	Glasgow
History	Sister to **CLAN MACLAREN (II), CLAN MACLEOD (IV)** and **CLAN MACLAY.**

1947, June 2: launched for Clan Line Steamers Ltd.

1956, July 29: rescued the crew of the sail training ship **MOYANA**, belonging to the Southampton School of Navigation, Warsash, England. A painting of this rescue hangs at the College, now Warsash Maritime Centre. The rescue took place in the Approaches to the English Channel. The **MOYANA** foundered 60 miles south of Plymouth.

1976: sold to Singapore Islands Lines (Pte) Ltd., Singapore. Renamed **SENTOSA ISLAND**.

Disposal

1979, June 16: demolition commenced at Kaohsiung, Taiwan, by Long Jong Industry Co. Ltd.

Photo credit   WSPL.

CLAN MACFARLANE (III)

Ex Names	**JOHN BRANCH** - 1943 launched as **SAMBRIAN** - 1947
Official Number	169716 (registered at London)
Signal Letters	BFNS/GCSW
GRT as built	7176
NRT	4380
Dimensions in feet	loa 441.7 x 57.0
Summer Draught	27' 9" at 10865 dwt.
Built by	North Carolina Shipbuilding Corporation
Year	1943/8 **At** Wilmington, North Carolina, USA
Yard Number	186 - the last Liberty type built at this yard.
Engine type	T3, 24½", 37", 70" - stroke 48" **Speed** 11
Built by	Vulcan Iron Works
At	Wilkes-Barre, Pennsylvania, USA.
History	Sister to **CLAN MACFADYEN (III).**

1943, August: completed for the MOWT as the Liberty ship **SAMBRIAN**. Operated by Cayzer Irvine & Co., Ltd.

1946, August 31: sailed from Port Said, Egypt, tail shaft broke and lost with her propeller. Five days later she was towed to Alexandria, Egypt, where a tail shaft and propeller were fitted having been taken from the wreck of the Liberty ship **THOMAS G. MASARYK**.

1947: purchased by Clan Line Steamers Ltd. Renamed **CLAN MACFARLANE**.

1961: sold to Vesta Maritime Corp., Beirut, Lebanon. Renamed **NICHOLAS**.

1961, October 10: driven ashore in a typhoon at Hachinoe, Honshu, Japan. Abandoned.

1961, October 27: refloated and taken to Hachinoe as a constructive total loss.

Disposal

1962, January 25: arrived at Yokosuka, Japan, to be broken up.

Photo credit   WSPL.

CLAN MACFADYEN (III)

Ex Name	SAMDERWENT - 1947
LR Number	5043320
Official Number	169959 (registered at London)
Signal Letters	MYRV/GCSR
GRT as built	7291
NRT	4380
Dimensions in feet	loa 441.7 x 57.0
Summer Draught	27' 9½"
Built by	New England Shipbuilding Corp.
Year	1944/3
At	Portland. Maine, USA
Yard Number	2224
Engine type	T3, 24½", 37", 70" - stroke 48"
Speed	11½
Built by	Springfield Machine & Foundry Co.
At	Springfield, Massachusetts, USA

History

1944, March: A Liberty ship delivered to the Ministry of War Transport, operated by Cayzer Irvine & Co. Ltd. as managers.

1947: acquired by Clan Line and renamed **CLAN MACFADYEN**.

1958: sold to Cia. Nav. Betacruz, Piraeus, Greece, (Liberian flag). Renamed **BETAVISTA.**

1968: sold to Thakur Shipping Co. Ltd., Bombay, India. Renamed **VARUNA DEVI.**

Disposal

1971, April 21: arrived at Kaohsiung, Taiwan, for breaking up.

Photo credit   D. Wittridge.

CLAN MACKELLAR (II)

Ex Name   **EMPIRE LANKESTER** - 1948
LR Number   502275
Official Number   180071 (registered at West Hartlepool)
Signal Letters   MQJK
GRT as built   7067
NRT   4844
Dimensions in feet   loa 446.3 x 56.2
Summer Draught   26' 9"
Built by   Wm. Gray & Co. Ltd.
Year   1944/4
At   West Hartlepool   **Yard Number** 1161
Engine type   T3, 24½", 39", 70", - stroke 48"   **Speed**   12
Built by   Central Marine Engine Works (Wm. Gray & Co. Ltd.)
At   West Hartlepool
History   Sister to **CLAN ANGUS, CLAN MACKENDRICK, CLAN ALLAN,**
CLAN MACKENZIE (IV). All built for the Ministry of War Transport.
1944, February 22: launched for the MOWT.
1944, April: completed and operated by J. Robinson & Sons (Stag Line), North Shields, managers.
1946: Clan Line became the charterer.
1948: acquired by Clan Line. Renamed **CLAN MACKELLAR.**
1961: transferred to King Line Ltd and sold to Mullion & Co. Ltd., Hong Kong. Registered at Gibraltar. Renamed **ARDGROOM**.
Disposal
1967, February 20: sold by Mullion & Co. Ltd. to Lee Sing Co.
On the same date arrived at Hong Kong to be broken up.
Photo credit   WSPL.

CLAN MACKINNON (III)

Ex Name   **EMPIRE DUNNET** - 1946
LR Number   520138
Official Number   180086
Signal Letters   GKLX
GRT as built   7372
NRT   5226
Dimensions in feet   loa 449.0 x 56.2   Summer Draught 26' 9" at 10100 dwt.
Built by Wm. Gray & Co. Ltd. **Year** 1945/9 **At** West Hartlepool **Yard Number** 1177
Engine type   T3, 24", 39", 70", - stroke 48" **Speed** 12
Built by   Central Marine Engine Works (Wm. Gray & Co. Ltd.)
At   West Hartlepool
History   Sister to **CLAN MACKINLAY (II), CLAN MACKAY (V),**
              CLAN MURRAY (IV) and CLAN MURDOCH (II).

1945, July 10: launched for the MOWT as the **EMPIRE DUNNET** and managed by Cayzer Irvine & Co., Ltd.
1946: acquired by Clan Line Steamers Ltd. Renamed **CLAN MACKINNON.**
1955: transferred to Houston Line as manager.
1957: reverted to Cayzer Irvine & Co., Ltd., as managers.
1958, June: chartered for one voyage to the Sri Lankan Navy.
1961: sold to Mullion & Co., Ltd., Hong Kong. Renamed **ARDROSS**.
1963: January: sold to Concordia Kinabatangan S. A., Panama. Renamed **LABUAN BAY**.
1967: March 20: went aground on Bancoran Island, Philippines, and refloated after four days.
1967: July 11: had a fire in her cargo.

Disposal
1967, October: broken up at Kaohsiung, Taiwan.

Photo credit   WSPL

CLAN MACKINLAY (II)

Ex Name	**EMPIRE FAWLEY** - 1946
Official Number	180221
Signal Letters	GJTC
GRT as built	7382
NRT	5295
Dimensions in feet	loa 449.0 x 56.3
Summer Draught	26' 9" at 10100 dwt.
Built by	J. Readhead & Sons Ltd.
Year	1945/6
At	South Shields
Yard Number	545
Engine type	T3, 24½", 39", 70", - stroke 48"
Speed	12
Built by	Vickers-Armstrong Ltd.
At	Barrow-in-Furness

History   Sister to **CLAN MACKINNON (II), CLAN MACKAY (V),
CLAN MURRAY (IV)** and **CLAN MURDOCH (II)**

1945, April 25: launched for the MOWT as **EMPIRE FAWLEY**, completed with Cayzer Irvine & Co. Ltd. as managers.
1946: acquired by Clan Line Steamers Ltd. Renamed **CLAN MACKINLAY (III)**.

Disposal
1967, November 2: arrived at Hong Kong for breaking up.
Photo credit   A. Duncan.

CLAN MACKAY (V)

Ex Name	**EMPIRE GUNFLEET** - 1946
Official Number	180223
Signal Letters	GKSX
GRT as built	7389
NRT	5255
Dimensions in feet	loa 449.0 x 56.3
Summer Draught	26' 9" at 10120 dwt.
Built by	J. Readhead & Sons Ltd.
Year	1945/11
At	South Shields
Yard Number	547
Engine type	T3, 24½", 39", 70", - stroke 48"
Speed	12
Built by	J. Readhead & Sons Ltd.
At	South Shields
History	Sister to **CLAN MACKINNON (II), CLAN MACKINLAY (II), CLAN MURRAY (IV)** and **CLAN MURDOCH (II).**

1945, August 8: launched for the MOWT as **EMPIRE GUNFLEET**, completed with Cayzer Irvine & Co. Ltd. as managers.

1946: acquired by Clan Line Steamers Ltd. Renamed **CLAN MACKAY (V)**.

1962: sold to Cia. De Nav. Victoria Neptuno S. A., Panama. Renamed **BABYLON.**

Disposal

1966, September 25: laid up at Hong Kong.

1966, December: sold to Ming Hing & Co., Hong Kong and broken up.

Photo credit   A. Duncan.

CLAN MURRAY (IV)

Ex Names	**EMPIRE LONGSTONE** - 1946	**HESPERIDES (IV)** - 1960
Official Number	180929 (registered at London)	
Signal Letters	GJSK	
GRT as built	7301	
NRT	5280	
Dimensions in feet	loa 449.0 x 56.3	
Summer Draught	26' 9¼"	
Built by	Shipbuilding Corp. Ltd. (Wear Branch)	
Year	1946/8	
At	Sunderland	
Yard Number	9	
Engine type	T3, 24½", 39", 70", - stroke 48"	
Speed	12	
Built by	George Clark (1938) Ltd.	
At	Sunderland	

History   Sister to **CLAN MACKINNON (III), CLAN MACKINLAY (II), CLAN MACKAY (V)** and **CLAN MURDOCH (II)**

1946, May 2: launched for the MOWT as **EMPIRE LONGSTONE**.
1946, August: completed as **HESPERIDES** with Houston Line Ltd. as managers.
1960: transferred to Clan Line Steamers Ltd. Renamed **CLAN MURRAY (IV).**

Disposal
1962: broken up at Osaka, Japan.
Photo credit   A. Duncan.

CLAN MACLENNAN

LR Number	5075189
Official Number	182080
Signal Letters	GSYP
GRT as built	6366
NRT	3168
Dimensions in feet	loa 466.0 x 60.8
Summer Draught	26' 0¾" at 8814 dwt.
Built by	Greenock Dockyard Co. Ltd.
Year	1947/12
At	Greenock
Yard Number	466
Engine type	Steam turbines x 3, geared to a single screw.
Speed	15
Built by	D. Rowan & Co. Ltd.
At	Glasgow

History   Sister to **CLAN MACLACHLAN (II).**
1947, September 16: launched for Clan Line Steamers Ltd.
1971: transferred to King Line from Clan Line, but she had previously been nominally in the Hector Whaling Company fleet.

Disposal
1971, September 21: delivered to shipbreakers at Shanghai, China.

Photo credit   M. Lindsay

CLAN MACLEOD (IV)

LR Number   5075191
Official Number   182090
Signal Letters   GSZC
GRT as built   6073
NRT   3367
Dimensions in feet loa 466.0 x 60.9
Summer Draught   26' 0¾" at 8786 dwt.
Built by   Greenock Dockyard Co. Ltd.
Year 1947/8   **At** Greenock   **Yard Number**   467
Engine type   Doxford, 2 stroke, single acting, 6 cylinders.
Speed   15
Built by   Barclay, Curle & Co. Ltd.
At   Glasgow
History   Sister to **CLAN MACLAREN (II), CLAN MACLEAN (III)**
                       and **CLAN MACLAY.**

1948, February 13: launched for Clan Line Steamers Ltd.

1971, November/December: Detained for 16 days off Madras, India, during the Indian-Pakistan War as she was carrying cargo destined for East Pakistan, now Bangladesh.

1972, February 25: called at Durban for bunkers and stores. Almost all items of food and drink were totally exhausted, due to the shortage of goods in India because of the War.

1972, August 7: discharged a cargo of White rhinoceros at Southend anchorage. The dockers who were on strike agreed to work for "humanitarian reasons".

1976: sold to Alligator Shipping Co. Ltd., Limassol, Cyprus. Renamed **PAPAJI.**

Disposal

1978: arrived at Gadani Beach, Pakistan, for breaking up.

Photo credit   A. J. Blackler.

CLAN MACLEOD

Discharging Rhino @ Southend
7-8-1972 CLAN MACLEOD
301c-3-29 © A J Blackler

31

CLAN DAVIDSON (II)

Ex Name	**HMS BONAVENTURE** - 1947
Official Number	182100 (registered on transfer to the Merchant Navy)
Signal Letters	MAWU
GRT as rebuilt	8067
NRT	3697
Dimensions in feet	loa 487.0 x 63.0
Summer Draught	28' 4½" at 9722 dwt.
Built by	Greenock Dockyard Co. Ltd.
Year	1943/1
At	Greenock
Yard Number	452
Engine type	T3 x 2, 26", 42", 68"- stroke 48" + a LP turbine + DR geared to twin shafts.
Speed	16
Built by	J. G. Kincaid & Co. Ltd.
At	Greenock

History

1942, October 27: launched and requisitioned by the Admiralty.

1943, January 23: commissioned as a midget submarine depot ship in Scotland, named **HMS BONAVENTURE.**

1947: rebuilt by her builders, with passenger accommodation.

1948: returned to Clan Line. Renamed **CLAN DAVIDSON.**

1948, November 11: sailed from Birkenhead on her maiden voyage as a merchant ship.

1961: transferred to King Line Ltd.

Disposal

1961, December 25: arrived at Hong Kong for breaking up.

Photo credit   A. Duncan & Company postcards.

CLAN MACLAY

LR Number	5075165
Official Number	182109
Signal Letters	GSTB
GRT as built	6075
NRT	3367
Dimensions in feet	loa 466.0 x 60.9
Summer Draught	26' 0¾" at 8786 dwt.
Built by	Greenock Dockyard Co. Ltd.
Year	1949/3
At	Greenock
Yard Number	468
Engine type	Doxford, 2 stroke, single acting, 6 cylinders.
Speed	15
Built by	Barclay, Curle & Co. Ltd.
At	Glasgow

History Sister to **CLAN MACLEOD (IV), CLAN MACLAREN (II)** and **CLAN MACLEAN (III).**

1948, May 7: launched for Clan Line Steamers Ltd.

1976: transferred to King Line Ltd.

1976: sold to Climax Shipping Corp., Panama. Renamed **CLIMAX ANGELOS.**

1979: renamed **ANGELOS** for the voyage to the breakers.

Disposal

1979: June: broken up at Kaosiung, Taiwan, by Keun Hwa Steel Works & Enterprise Ltd.

Photo credit M. Lindsay

34

CLAN MACTAGGART (II)

LR Number	5075220
Official Number	182111
Signal Letters	GUBC
GRT as built	8035
NRT	3924
Dimensions in feet	loa 505.0 x 65.7
Summer Draught	28' 3½" at 10800 dwt.
Built by	Greenock Dockyard Co. Ltd.
Year	1949/3
At	Greenock
Yard Number	469
Engine type	Steam turbines x 6, double reduction geared to twin shafts.
Speed	16¾
Built by	Parsons Marine Turbine Co. Ltd.
At	Wallsend-on-Tyne.

History Sister to **CLAN MACTAVISH (II)**. These ships had 1 x 125 ton SWL derrick.
1948, October 8: launched for Clan Line Steamers Ltd.
1971: transferred to King Line Ltd.

Disposal
1971: sold to Eduardo Varela.
1971, November 12: arrived at Bilbao, Spain, for breaking up.

Photo credit D. Wittridge.

CLAN MACTAVISH (III)

LR Number	5075232
Official Number	182124
Signal Letters	GUBB
GRT as built	8035
NRT	3926
Dimensions in feet	loa 505.5 x 65.7
Summer Draught	28' 3½ at 10800 dwt.
Built by	Greenock Dockyard Co. Ltd.
Year	1949/6
At	Greenock
Yard Number	470
Engine type	Steam turbines x 6, geared to twin shafts.
Speed	16.75
Built by	Parsons Marine Turbine Co. Ltd.
At	Wallsend-on-Tyne

History   Sister to **CLAN MACTAGGART (II).**
1949, March 2: launched for Clan Line Steamers Ltd.

Disposal
1971, October 27: delivered to breakers at Whampoa, China.

Photo credit   Clan Line postcard.

CLAN SHAW (III)

LR Number	533498
Official Number	182140
Signal Letters	GBYW
GRT as built	8101
NRT	4659
Dimensions in feet	loa 512.6 x 66.3
Summer Draught	28' 0½" at 10955 dwt.
Built by	Greenock Dockyard Co. Ltd.
Year	1950/1
At	Greenock
Yard Number	471
Engine type	Steam turbines x 3, double reduction geared to a single screw.
Speed	17
Built by	Parsons Marine Turbine Co. Ltd.
At	Wallsend-on-Tyne
History	Sister to **CLAN SINCLAIR (III) CLAN SUTHERLAND (III)** and **CLAN STEWART.** They had accommodation for 12 passengers.

1949, August 23: launched for Clan Line Steamers Ltd.

1953. June 15: represented Clan Line at the Coronation Review at Spithead, Solent.

1960, January: transferred to Springbok Line, South Africa. Renamed **STEENBOK.**

1961: transferred to Safmarine. Renamed **SOUTH AFRICAN SEAFARER.**

1966: transferred back to Springbok Line, (Safmarine, managed). Renamed **S. A. SEAFARER.**

Disposal

1966, July 1: wrecked on Green Point, Cape Town, South Africa. 63 crew and 12 passengers were rescued by helicopter. The ship broke up.

Photo credit   D. Wittridge.

CLAN SINCLAIR (III)

LR Number	5335008
Official Number	182148
Signal Letters	GFWW
GRT as built	8386
NRT	4445
Dimensions in feet	loa 512.6 x 66.3
Summer Draught	27' 11½" at 11000 dwt.
Built by	Greenock Dockyard Co. Ltd.
Year	1950/4
At	Greenock
Yard Number	472
Engine type	Steam turbines x 3, double reduction geared to a single screw.
Speed	17
Built by	Parsons Marine Turbine Co. Ltd.
At	Wallsend-on-Tyne
History	Sister to **CLAN SHAW (III), CLAN SUTHERLAND (III)** and **CLAN STEWART.**

1960: transferred to Springbok Line. Renamed **BOSBOK.**

1961: transferred to Safmarine management. Renamed **SOUTH AFRICAN STATESMAN**.

1966: transferred back to Springbok Line. Name shortened to **S. A. STATESMAN**.

Disposal

1972, November 3: arrived at Kaohsiung, Taiwan, for breaking up by Li Chong Steel Corp.

Photo credit   A. Duncan.

CLAN SUTHERLAND (II)

LR Number	5075282
Official Number	182167
Signal Letters	GFWZ
GRT as built	8436
NRT	4434
Dimensions in feet	loa 512.6 x 66.3
Summer Draught	27' 11½" at 10870 dwt.
Built by	Greenock Dockyard Co. Ltd.
Year	1951/3　　　**At** Greenock　　**Yard Number**　475
Engine type	Steam turbines x 3, double reduction geared to a single screw.
Speed	17
Built by	Parsons Marine Turbine Co. Ltd.
At	Wallsend-on-Tyne
History	Sister to **CLAN SHAW (III), CLAN SINCLAIR (III)** and **CLAN STEWART.**

She had the heaviest SWL derrick in the fleet at 165 tons.

1971: transferred to King Line Ltd.

Disposal

1971, November 10: arrived at Hsingkang, China, for scrapping by China National Machinery Import & Export Corp., but she may have been resold to China Ocean Shipping Co. (COSCO) for further trading.

*Note: This ship was photographed as the Chinese ship **ZHAN DOU 3** in July 1979 (without her heavy lift derrick) and she was seen again as a depot ship in China in 1984, despite having been sold for scrap in 1971. (Photo: M. A. Berger, Switzerland 1979).*

Photo credit　　WSPL + M. A. Berger.

CLAN MACINTOSH (III)

LR Number	5075115
Official Number	184959
Signal Letters	GMTJ
GRT as built	6558
NRT	3605
Dimensions in feet	loa 471.0 x 60.7
Summer Draught	26' 1½" at 9118 dwt.
Built by	John Brown & Co. (Clydebank) Ltd.
Year	1951/11
At	Clydebank
Yard Number	665
Engine type	Doxford, 2 stroke, single acting, 6 cylinders.
Speed	15¼
Built by	John Brown & Co. (Clydebank) Ltd.
At	Clydebank

History   Sister to **CLAN MACINTYRE (III)** and **CLAN MACINNES (III).**
1978: sold to Sanil Shipping Co. Ltd., Hong Kong. Renamed **SANIL.**

Disposal
1980, August 28: arrived at Bombay, India - for breaking up by Haryana Steel Co.
1981, January: demolition work commenced.

Photo credit   M. Lindsay

CLAN MACINTYRE (III)

LR Number   5075127
Official Number   184963
Signal Letters   MNMM
GRT as built   6560
NRT   3602
Dimensions in feet loa 471.0 x 60.7
Summer Draught   26' 1½" at 9110 dwt.
Built by   John Brown & Co. (Clydebank) Ltd.
Year   1952/3
At   Clydebank
Yard Number   666
Engine type   Doxford, 2 stroke, single acting, 6 cylinders.
Speed   15.25
Built by   John Brown & Co. (Clydebank) Ltd.
At   Clydebank

History   Sister to **CLAN MACINTOSH (III)** and **CLAN MACINNES (III).**
1976: transferred to King Line Ltd.
1976: sold to Renown Bay Shipping Co., Panama, (Wallem Group, Hong Kong).
Renamed **EASTERN EXPRESS.**

Disposal
1979, December 22: grounded during a gale at Marina di Carrara, Italy. Declared a constructive total loss.

Photo credit   Anon.

SCOTTISH EAGLE (I)

LR Number	5399080
Official Number	184968
Signal Letters	MMVX
GRT as built	11193
NRT	6367
Dimensions in feet	loa 547.3 x 69.9
Summer Draught	29' 11" at 15710 dwt.
Built by	Swan, Hunter & Wigham Richardson Ltd.
Year	1952/5
At	Newcastle
Yard Number	1888
Engine type	Doxford, 2 stroke, single acting, 6 cylinders.
Speed	13½
Built by	Swan, Hunter & Wigham Richardson Ltd.
At	Newcastle

History   Sister to **SCOTTISH LION (I)** and **SCOTTISH HAWK.**
The funnel colours of Scottish Tankers Ltd. were the same as Clan Line Steamers, except the narrow black band was blue. Scottish Tankers Ltd. was the tanker arm of the fleet managed by Cayzer Irvine & Co. Ltd.
1952, February 25: launched for Scottish Tankers Ltd., (Cayzer Irvine & Co. Ltd.).
1962: sold to Gulf Steamships Ltd., Pakistan. Renamed **ZOHRA**.

Disposal
1969, December 31: arrived at Karachi, Pakistan, prior to breaking up.
Photo credit   A. Duncan.

51

CLAN MACINNES (III)

LR Number	5075103
Official Number	184974
Signal Letters	GNWG
GRT as built	6588
NRT	3621
Dimensions in feet	loa 471.0 x 60.7
Summer Draught	26' 1½" at 8996 dwt.
Built by	Greenock Dockyard Co. Ltd.
Year	1952/7
At	Greenock
Yard Number	478
Engine type	Doxford, 2 stroke, single acting, 6 cylinders.
Speed	15
Built by	John Brown & Co. Ltd.
At	Clydebank

History   Sister to **CLAN MACINTOSH (III)** and **CLAN MACINTYRE (III).**
1952, April 9: launched for Clan Line Steamers Ltd.
1978: sold to Ali Khalifa Mirchandani Shipping Co. Ltd., Kuwait. Renamed **ATHOUB.**
1979, October 15: sold to Lung Ching Steel Enterprise Co. Ltd. and arrived at Kaohsiung, Taiwan, for breaking up by them.

Disposal
1979, October 16: demolition work commenced.
Photo credit   D. Wittridge.

CLAN STEWART / KINPURNIE CASTLE (I)

LR Number   5188314

Official Number   185001

Signal Letters   GQKT - GJQA on return to British flag.

GRT as built   8163

NRT   4587

Dimensions in feet   loa 512.6 x 66.3

Summer Draught   28' 0" at 11070 dwt.

Built by   Greenock Dockyard Co. Ltd.

Year   1954/2

At   Greenock

Yard Number   481

Engine type   Steam turbines x 3, double reduction geared to single screw.

Speed   15

Built by   Parsons Marine Turbine Co. Ltd.

At   Wallsend-on-Tyne

History   Sister to **CLAN SHAW (III), CLAN SINCLAIR (III),** and **CLAN SUTHERLAND (II).**

1953, October 22: launched. She was fitted with a 105 tons SWL derrick.

1961: transferred to Safmarine, Cape Town. Renamed **SOUTH AFRICAN SCULPTOR.**

1962: reverted to Clan Line. Renamed **KINPURNIE CASTLE (I)** and placed on an internal charter for Union-Castle service.

1967: transferred to King Line Ltd.

1967: sold to Astro Firme Cia. Nav. S. A., Greece. Renamed **HELLENIC MED.**

Disposal

1978, March: arrived at Gadani Beach, Pakistan, for breaking up.

Photo credit   D. Wittridge.

CLAN ROBERTSON (III)

LR Number	5334999
Official Number	185012
Signal Letters	GRQQ
GRT as built	7878
NRT	4107
Dimensions in feet	loa 502.8 x 65.7
Summer Draught	28' 3½" at 10802 dwt.
Built by	Greenock Dockyard Co. Ltd.
Year	1954/6
At	Greenock
Yard Number	482
Engine type	Steam turbines x 3, double reduction geared to a single screw.
Speed	17
Built by	Parsons Marine Turbine Co. Ltd.
At	Wallsend-on-Tyne
History	Sister to **CLAN ROSS (III)**.

1954, March 17: launched for Clan Line Steamers Ltd.

1959: transferred to Bullard, King & Co., London. Renamed **UMZINTO**.

1960: transferred to Springbok Line, Cape Town, South Africa. Renamed **ROOIBOK**.

1961: transferred to Safmarine management. Renamed **SOUTH AFRICAN SHIPPER**.

1966: transferred back to Springbok Line (Safmarine, managers).

Name shortened to **S. A. SHIPPER.**

Disposal

1975, November 26: arrived at Kaohsiung, Taiwan, for scrapping.

1975: December 27: demolition commenced by Sing Chen Yung Iron & Steel Corp.

Photo credit   WSPL

SCOTTISH HAWK

LR Number   5315826
Official Number   185020
Signal Letters   GRKC
GRT as built   11148
NRT   6185
Dimensions in feet   loa 546.6 x 69.3
Summer Draught   29' 10½" at 16360 dwt.
Built by Greenock Dockyard Co. Ltd. **Year** 1955/3 **At** Greenock **Yard Number** 483
Engine type   Doxford, 2 stroke, single acting, 6 cylinders.
Speed   13¾
Built by   Wallsend Slipway Co. Ltd.
At   Wallsend-on-Tyne
History   Sister to **SCOTTISH LION (I)** and **SCOTTISH EAGLE.**
Built for Scottish Tankers Ltd, part of the Cayzer Irvine Group.
1954, November 11: launched for Scottish Tanker Co. Ltd.
1965: sold to Marguardia Cia. Nav. S. A., Greece. Renamed **ANYTOS.**
1966: transferred to the Cypriot flag, retaining her name.
1967: transferred to Agenor Shipping Co., Cyprus. Retained name.
1970: sold to Marathnodromous Cia. Nav. S. A., Piraeus, Greece. Renamed **AEGIS PEACE**.
Disposal
1971, April 14: grounded at Alexandria, Egypt. Refloated and grounded again in a storm the next night. She suffered severe bottom damage.
1971, April 25: refloated and towed into port.
1972, January 9: left Alexandria under tow, bound for Valencia, Spain.
1972, January 22: arrived at Valencia for breaking up.
Photo credit   A. Duncan

CLAN ROSS (III) / KINNAIRD CASTLE

LR Number	5188209
Official Number	185040
Signal Letters	GVBV - GJPU on return to British flag.
GRT as built	7698
NRT	4263
Dimensions in feet	loa 503.0 x 65.5
Summer Draught	27' 3" at 10075 dwt.
Built by	Greenock Dockyard Co. Ltd.
Year	1956/4
At	Greenock
Yard Number	487
Engine type	Steam turbines x 3, double reduction geared to single screw.
Speed	17
Built by	Parsons Marine Turbine Co. Ltd
At	Wallsend-on-Tyne

History Sister to **CLAN ROBERTSON (III).** Both ships were fitted for 12 passengers.
1956, January 17: launched for Clan Line Steamers Ltd.
1961: transferred to Safmarine, Cape Town. Renamed **SOUTH AFRICAN SCIENTIST.**
1962, June 1: reverted to Clan Line for Union-Castle operations. Renamed **KINNAIRD CASTLE.**
The passenger accommodation was used by 12 cadets.
1968: transferred to King Line Ltd., chartered by Union-Castle Line.
1975: sold by King Line Ltd. to Dasonab Nav. S. A., Panama. Renamed **NAZEER.**
Disposal
1978, April: arrived at Gadani Beach, Pakistan for breaking up.
Photo credit Real Photo Co.

2755

ARGYLLSHIRE (ll)

LR Number	5023605
Official Number	185047
Signal Letters	GVBX
GRT as built	9299
NRT	5267
Dimensions in feet	loa 534.9 x 69.3
Summer Draught	28' 4¼" at 11240 dwt.
Built by	Greenock Dockyard Co. Ltd.
Year	1956/10
At	Greenock
Yard Number	486
Engine type	Steam turbines x 3, double reduction geared to a single screw.
Speed	16 ¾
Built by	Parson's Marine Turbine Co. Ltd.
At	Wallsend-on-Tyne

History   Sister to **AYRSHIRE (II).**

Built for Clan Line's Australian meat and wool trade. They had refrigerated holds and carried up to 12 passengers. They were equipped with 1 x 105 and 2 x 40 tons SWL derricks.

1960: transferred to Scottish Shire Line Ltd.

1975: sold to Gulf East Marine Inc., Monrovia, Liberia. Renamed **SCHIVAGO.**

Disposal

1977, August: arrived Gadani Beach, Pakistan for breaking up.

Photo credit   M.Lindsay

63

KING ARTHUR (V)

LR Number	5187499
Official Number	185856 (registered at London)
Signal Letters	GQAX
GRT as built	5883
NRT	3346
Dimensions in feet	loa 466.5 x 52.2
Summer Draught	25' 9" at 9570 dwt.

Built by   Harland & Wolff Ltd. **Year**   1953/3 **At**   Belfast   **Yard Number**   1462

Engine type   Harland & Wolff, 4 stroke, single acting, 6 cylinders.

Speed   12½ **Built by**   Harland & Wolff Ltd. **At** Belfast

History   Sister to **KING ALEXANDER, KING CHARLES (I), KING GEORGE (I)** and **KING MALCOLM.**

1952, November 19: launched for King Line Ltd. (part of Union-Castle R.M.S.S. Co. Ltd), London.

1956: acquired by Cayzer Irvine & Co. Ltd., when the Union-Castle Group was merged into the company.

1959, November: transferred to Clan Line Steamers Ltd.

1963, January: reverted to King Line Ltd.

1972, May: sold to Kition Cia. Nav. (Alassia S. S. Co. Ltd., managers), Limassol, Cyprus. Renamed **TOULLA.**

1980: renamed **DESPO**. Same owners.

1980: sold to Basco Enterprises Pte. Ltd., Panama. Renamed **PEARL RAINBOW.**

1981: sold to Greenleaf Nav. Co., Panama. Renamed **GREENLEAF**.

Disposal

1983, June 14: departed Singapore for Chittagong, Bangladesh for scrapping.

1983, July 30: demolition commenced by Emzed Enterprises at Dhaka, Bangladesh.

Photo credit   Harland & Wolff Ltd. & A. J. Blackler

KING CHARLES (I)

LR Number	5187504
Official Number	187593 (registered at London)
Signal Letters	GWKL
GRT as built	5993
NRT	3296
Dimensions in feet	loa 466.5 x 59.2
Summer Draught	25' 9" at 9570 dwt.
Built by	Harland & Wolff Ltd.
Year	1957/6 **At** Belfast **Yard Number** 1556
Engine type	Harland & Wolff, 4 stroke single acting, 6 cylinders. **Speed** 12½
Built by	Harland & Wolff Ltd.
At	Belfast
History	Sister to **KING ALEXANDER, KING GEORGE (I), KING MALCOLM,** and **KING ARTHUR (V)**. All were built for King Line Ltd., part of the Union-Castle Group before 1956.

1957, March 15: launched for King Line Ltd., (Cayzer Irvine & Co. Ltd., managers).

1959, November: transferred to Clan Line Steamers Ltd.

1970: transferred to Houston Line Ltd.

1973, February: sold to Cephissos Shipping Co. Ltd., Cyprus, (Aegis Shipping Co. Ltd., managers). Renamed **AEGIS MIGHT**.

1976: transferred to Marmari Shipping Corporation Ltd., Greece, (same managers). Retained name.

Disposal

1979: sold by Marmari Shipping Corporation Ltd., to Taiwanese shipbreakers.

1979, July 27: arrived at Kaohsiung for breaking up.

1979, August 6: demolition commenced by Kao Yung Steel Enterprise Co.

Photo credit   M. Lindsay

AYRSHIRE (III)

Official Number	300171
Signal Letters	GVBW
GRT as built	9360
NRT	5302
Dimensions in feet	loa 534.9 x 69.2
Summer Draught	28' 4½" at 11240 dwt.
Built by	Greenock Dockyard Co. Ltd.
Year	1957/5 **At** Greenock **Yard Number** 488
Engine type	Steam turbines x 3, double reduction geared to a single screw.
Speed	16¾
Built by	Parsons Marine Turbine Co. Ltd. **At** Wallsend-on-Tyne
History	Sister to **ARGYLLSHIRE (II)**.

1956, October 19: launched for Clan Line Steamers Ltd., for the Australian refrigerated cargo trade. She had accommodation for 12 passengers.

1960: transferred to Scottish Shire Line, (Turnbull, Martin, managers, part of the British & Commonwealth Group).

1965, March 23: **AYRSHIRE** struck an uncharted rock off Abd Al Kuri Island near Socotra. She was beached, some cargo was salvaged, but the ship became a total loss. The passengers were transferred to the cadetship, **CLAN MALCOLM (II),** whose 12 cadets and their training officer were transferred to the **AYRSHIRE**. According to my notes written at the time, the **CLAN MALCOLM** took the seven passengers and six dogs from the **AYRSHIRE** in exchange. (I was 3rd Mate of the **CLAN MALCOLM**).

Disposal

1965, April 26: refloated but a few minutes later she was swept aground again, by strong currents and wind. She was abandoned the next day as a total loss.

Photo credit Clan Line.

CLAN MALCOLM (II)

LR Number	5075244
Official Number	300181
Signal Letters	GVWQ
GRT as built	7686
NRT	4171
Dimensions in feet	loa 502.7 x 65.7
Summer Draught	27' 3" at 9810 dwt.
Built by	Greenock Dockyard Co. Ltd.
Year	1957/8 **At** Greenock
Yard Number	490
Engine type	Doxford, 2 stroke single acting, 6 cylinders.
Speed	16¼
Built by	Wallsend Slipway & Engine Co. Ltd.
At	Wallsend-on-Tyne

History   Sister to **CLAN MATHESON (V)** and **CLAN MENZIES (III)**.
They were built with accommodation for 12 passengers.
1965, March 26: transferred seven passengers, six dogs and the ship's papers from the company ship **AYRSHIRE**, which had been beached on Abd Al Kuri Island off Socotra, after she had hit an uncharted rock, in fine weather. The **CLAN MALCOLM** was a cadet ship and her 12 cadets and the training officer were transferred to the **AYRSHIRE** to help with salvage operations, which turned out to be largely unsuccessful.
1979: sold to Bective Shipping Corp., Panama, with the **CLAN MENZIES (III).**
Renamed **TRINITY FAIR.**

Disposal
1979, May 25: left Bangkok, Thailand, for Shanghai, China, for breaking up.

Photo credit   M. Lindsay

70

SCOTTISH PTARMIGAN

LR Number	5315876
Official Number	300190
Signal Letters	GTPP
GRT as built	12685
NRT	7100
Dimensions in feet	loa 559.0 x 72.3
Summer Draught	30' 2" at 18300 dwt.
Built by	John Brown & Co. (Clydebank) Ltd.
Year	1958/1 **At** Clydebank **Yard Number** 701
Engine type	Doxford, 2 stroke single acting, 6 cylinders. **Speed** 13½
Built by	John Brown & Co. (Clydebank) Ltd.
At `	Clydebank

History

1957, October 24: Oil tanker launched for Scottish Tankers (Cayzer Irvine subsidiary, Thompson S. S. Co. Ltd., managers).

1968: sold to Cia. de Nav. Alheli, S. A., Monrovia, Liberia. Renamed **MARKAB.**

1970: sold to N. J. Vardinoyannis, Piraeus, Greece. Renamed **ELENI V.**

Disposal

1978, May 6: cut in two, just forward of the bridge, when in collision with **ROSELINE**, off Haisbro Lightship. The aft end was towed to Europoort, Holland, and discharged.

The fore part sank, in shallow water, leaking oil, which caused considerable pollution along England's East Coast.

1978, May 15: the fore part was refloated. It was later sunk by explosives in deeper water.

1978, July 15: the aft part was sold and towed to Santander, Spain, for scrapping, arriving there on July 20.

Photo credit A. Duncan.

CLAN MENZIES (III)

LR Number	5075268
Official Number	300200
Signal Letters	MXWD
GRT as built	7685
NRT	4180
Dimensions in feet	loa 502.7 x 65.7
Summer Draught	27' 3" at 9830 dwt.
Built by	Greenock Dockyard Co. Ltd
Year	1958/5
At	Greenock
Yard Number	491
Engine type	Doxford, 2 stroke, single acting, 6 cylinders.
Speed	16¼
Built by	Wallsend Slipway & Engine Co. Ltd.
At	Wallsend-on-Tyne

History   Sister to **CLAN MALCOLM (II)** and **CLAN MATHESON (V)**.
1958, January 22: launched for Clan Line Steamers Ltd.
1979: sold to Bective Shipping, Panama. Renamed **TRINITY SPLENDOUR**.
1980: became **XING LONG** of China Ocean Shipping Co., (COSCO), China.

Disposal
1993: untraced; out of Lloyd's Register of Ships.

Photo credit   Real Photo Co.

75

CLAN MACIVER (III)

LR Number	5075139
Official Number	300214
Signal Letters	GXBX
GRT as built	7350
NRT	3686
Dimensions in feet	loa 494.0 x 61.7
Summer Draught	26' 4¼" at 9780 dwt.
Built by	Greenock Dockyard Co. Ltd.
Year	1958/11
At	Greenock
Yard Number	492
Engine type	Doxford, 2 stroke, single acting, 5 cylinders.
Speed	13¾
Built by	Barclay, Curle & Co. Ltd.
At	Whiteinch, Glasgow

History Sister to **CLAN MACINDOE (II)** and **CLAN MACILWRAITH (II)**.
1958, June 23: launched for Clan Line Steamers Ltd. The first of a new type of company ship with 4 hatches forward of the bridge and 1 aft.
1979: sold to Quin Ace Maritime S. A., Panama. Renamed **TRINITY PRIDE.**

Disposal
1980, January 30: departed Hong Kong for Shanghai, China, for scrapping by Chinese shipbreakers.
1980, February 9: delivered to shipbreakers at Shanghai.
Photo credit   M. Lindsay

HECTOR HERON

LR Number	5145178
Official Number	300885 (registered at London)
Signal Letters	GBZH
GRT as built	12795
NRT	7659
Dimensions in feet	loa 560.0 x 69.9
Summer Draught	30' 8¼" at 18650 dwt.

Built by   Arsenal do Alfeite

Year   1959/5   **At** Alfeite, Portugal   **Yard Number** C41

Engine type   Götaverken, 2 stroke, single acting, 8 cylinders.   **Speed** 16

Built by   Uddevallavarvet AB   **At** Uddevalla, Sweden

History 1959, January 10: launched for Hector Whaling Ltd., London (Krohe-Hansen, managers), as a fuel oil/stores tanker for the company's whale catchers and returning with whale oil. She was fitted with dual lines for separation, one hold forward and seven derricks.

1962: Hector Whaling came into the Cayzer Irvine organisation and the ship was placed in the fleet of Scottish Tankers Ltd., (Huntley, Cook & Co. Ltd., managers), but retained Hector Whaling livery.

1975: sold to Armadores Maiverda S. A., Panama. Renamed **MARIHERON.**

1979, June 12: caught fire and grounded after a collision with **BRUCE BINTAN** (Bintan Shipcorp) in the Musi River, Sumatra.

1979, June 25: refloated and anchored at Palembang, Indonesia.

1979, August 27: sold to Loy Kee Shipbreaker and Transportation Co., Hong Kong.

Disposal

1979, September 12: after having been sold again she arrived at Kaohsiung, Taiwan, for breaking up.

Photo credit   A. J. Blackler & J. K. De Vries

CLAN MACINDOE (II)

LR Number	5075098
Official Number	301401
Signal Letters	GFLH
GRT as built	7395
NRT	3754
Dimensions in feet	loa 492.5 x 61.7
Summer Draught	26' 4¼" at 10272 dwt.
Built by	John Brown & Co. (Clydebank) Ltd.
Year	1959/11
At	Clydebank
Yard Number	712
Engine type	Doxford, 2 stroke, single acting, 5 cylinders.
Speed	15
Built by	John Brown & Co. (Clydebank) Ltd.
At	Clydebank
History	Sister to **CLAN MACIVER (III)** and **CLAN MACILWRAITH (II).**

1959, August 20: launched for Neptune Shipping Co., Hamilton, Bermuda, (Cayzer Irvine & Co. Ltd., managers), registered at Glasgow. The Neptune Shipping Co. was part of the British & Commonwealth Group.

1979: sold to Gulf Shipping Lines Ltd., Glasgow. Renamed **GULF HERON**, retained Glasgow registry.

Disposal

1980, September:during the Iran-Iraq War she was hit by shells in the Shatt-al-Arab and abandoned. *Lloyd's Register of Ships for 1985 states that she was "delayed in the Shatt-al-Arab".*

Photo credit   WSPL

CLAN MACILWRAITH (II)

LR Number	5075086
Official Number	301428
Signal Letters	GHDL
GRT as built	7354
NRT	3690
Dimensions in feet	loa 494.0 x 61.6
Summer Draught	26' 4¼" at 9990 dwt.
Built by	Greenock Dockyard Co. Ltd.
Year	1960/12
At	Greenock
Yard Number	496
Engine type	Doxford, 2 stroke, single acting, 5 cylinders.
Speed	14
Built by	Wallsend Slipway & Engine Co. Ltd.
At	Wallsend-on-Tyne
History	Sister to **CLAN MACIVER (III)** and **CLAN MACINDOE (II)**.

1960, May 27: launched for Clan Line Steamers Ltd.

1979: sold to Guan Guan Shipping (Pte) Ltd., Singapore. Renamed **GOLDEN CITY.**

1986, July 17: suffered a fire in No. 1 hold. She was in the Malacca Straits on a voyage from Colombo, Sri Lanka, to Singapore.

1986, July 24: arrived under tow at Singapore to discharge her cargo. The ship was found to be beyond economical repair.

Disposal

1986, October 21: scrapping commenced at Jurong, Singapore, by National Shipbreakers (Pte.) Ltd.

Photo credit   M. Lindsay

CLAN FERGUSSON

LR Number	5074965
Official Number	301439
Signal Letters	GHMV
GRT as built	9242
NRT	4965
Dimensions in feet	loa 496.6 x 62.4
Summer Draught	28' 2½" at 11920 dwt.
Built by	Swan, Hunter & Wigham Richardson Ltd.
Year	1961/4
At	Wallsend-on-Tyne
Yard Number	1917
Engine type	Sulzer, 2 stroke single acting, 6 cylinders.
Speed	16
Built by	Wallsend Slipway & Engineering Co. Ltd.
At	Wallsend-on-Tyne
History	Sister to **CLAN FORBES (IV), CLAN FRASER (IV), CLAN FARQUHARSON and CLAN FINLAY**. Known as the CLAN F's. These ships were fitted with 1 x 80 ton SWL derrick.

1960, November 3: launched for Clan Line Steamers Ltd.
1965: sold to Scindia Steam Navigation Co. Ltd., India, along with **CLAN FRASER**. Renamed **JALAPANKHI**.

Disposal

1983, February 5: arrived at Bombay, India, for breaking up there.

Photo credit   A. Duncan.

CLAN MACNAB (IV)

LR Number	5075206
Official Number	301448
Signal Letters	GHJH
GRT as built	9428
NRT	4995
Dimensions in feet	loa 506.5 x 61.7
Summer Draught	26' 7" at 10600 dwt.
Built by	Greenock Dockyard Co. Ltd.
Year	1961/5
At	Greenock
Yard Number	497
Engine type	Doxford, 2 stroke, single acting, 6 cylinders.
Speed	15¾
Built by	Wallsend Slipway & Engineering Co. Ltd.
At	Wallsend-on-Tyne

History   Sister to **CLAN MACNAIR (II)** and very similar to the CLAN F's and G's.
These ships had 1 x 80 tons and 1 x 40 tons S.W.L. derricks.
1961, October 26: launched for Neptune Shipping Co. Ltd., Bermuda. (Cayzer Irvine & Co. Ltd., managers). It was part of the British & Commonwealth Group. Registered at Glasgow.
1980: sold by Clan Line Steamers Ltd. to New Eagle Navigation S. A., Panama.
Renamed **NEW EAGLE.**

Disposal
1984, November 1: arrived Shanghai, China, for breaking up by Chinese shipbreakers.
Photo credit   A. Duncan.

CLAN FORBES (IV)

LR Number	5074989
Official Number	301454
Signal Letters	GHPW
GRT as built	9242
NRT	4965
Dimensions in feet	loa 496.6 x 62.4
Summer Draught	28' 2½" at 11290 dwt.
Built by	Swan, Hunter & Wigham Richardson Ltd.
Year	1961/6
At	Wallsend-on-Tyne
Yard Number	1919
Engine type	Sulzer, 2 stroke, single acting, 6 cylinders.
Speed	16
Built by	Wallsend Slipway & Engineering Co. Ltd.
At	Wallsend-on-Tyne

History   Sister to **CLAN FERGUSSON** and **CLAN FRASER (IV)**.
1961, March 2: launched for Clan Line Steamers Ltd.
1968: transferred to King Line Ltd.
1968: sold to Arya National Shipping Lines S. A Bandar Abbas, Iran. Renamed **ARYA MAN**.
1980: transferred to Islamic Republic of Iran Shipping Lines, Teheran, Iran, after nationalisation.
Renamed **IRAN HEMMAT.**

Disposal
1985, October 3: arrived at Alang, India, for scrap.
Photo credit   A. Duncan

CLAN FRASER (IV)

LR Number	5074991
Official Number	301461
Signal Letters	GHTE
GRT as built	9242
NRT	4965
Dimensions in feet	loa 496.6 x 62.4
Summer Draught	28' 2½" at 11920 dwt.
Built by	Swan, Hunter & Wigham Richardson Ltd.
Year	1961/9
At	Wallsend-on-Tyne
Yard Number	1921
Engine type	Sulzer, 2 stroke, single acting, 6 cylinders.
Speed	16
Built by	Wallsend Slipway & Engineering Co. Ltd.
At	Wallsend-on-Tyne

History   Sister to **CLAN FERGUSSON** and **CLAN FORBES (IV)** ; (Clan F's).
1961, July 27: launched for Clan Line Steamers Ltd.
1965: sold along with **CLAN FERGUSSON** to Scindia Steam Navigation Co., India, for a reported £850,000. Renamed **JALAPALAKA**.
1979, November 20: caught fire at Bombay, India.
Disposal
1980, November 17: sold to Jalyan Udyog, Calcutta, India, for demolition.
1980, December 24: demolition began at Darukhana, India.
Photo credit   WSPL

CLAN GRAHAM (IV)

LR Number   5075000
Official Number   301465
Signal Letters   GHTG
GRT as built   9308
NRT   5104
Dimensions in feet   loa 496.7 x 62.7
Summer Draught   28' 2¼" at 11900 dwt.
Built by   Greenock Dockyard Co. Ltd.
Year   1962/1
At   Greenock
Yard Number   498
Engine type   Sulzer, 2 stroke, single acting, 6 cylinders.   **Speed** 16
Built by   Barclay, Curle & Co. Ltd.
At   Glasgow
History   Sister to **CLAN GRANT (IV)** and very similar to the CLAN F's.
They were fitted with 1 x 80 tons SWL derrick.
1961, August 25: launched for Clan Line Steamers Ltd.
1969: transferred to King Line Ltd.
1977: reverted to Clan Line.
1981: sold to Scan Maritime Co., Panama. Renamed **MARIANNE.**
1983: sold to Kinsdale International S. A., Panama. Renamed **CANDELARIA**.
Disposal
1984, March 23: arrived Kaohsiung, Taiwan, for breaking up by Kuo Dar Steel & Iron Enterprise Co. Ltd.
1984, April 3: demolition work began.
Photo credit   M. Lindsay.

CLAN MACNAIR (II)

LR Number	5075218
Official Number	301468
Signal Letters	GHTR
GRT as built	9401
NRT	5025
Dimensions in feet	loa 506.2 x 61.7
Summer Draught	26' 6¾" at 10657 dwt.
Built by	John Brown & Co. (Clydebank) Ltd.
Year	1962/2
At	Clydebank
Yard Number	713
Engine type	Doxford, 2 stroke, single acting, 6 cylinders.
Speed	15¾
Built by	John Brown & Co. (Clydebank) Ltd.
At	Clydebank

History   Sister to **CLAN MACNAB (IV).**

1962, October 26: launched for Neptune Shipping Co Ltd., Bermuda, (Cayzer Irvine & Co. Ltd., managers). Neptune was part of the Group and she was registered at Glasgow.

1980, April: sold to Uni-Ocean Lines Pte., Singapore. Renamed **LICHIANG.**

Disposal

1987, April 7: arrived at Kaohsiung, Taiwan, for breaking up.

Photo credit   WSPL

CLAN FARQUHARSON

LR Number	5074953
Official Number	301475
Signal Letters	GIAQ
GRT as built	9242
NRT	4965
Dimensions in feet	loa 496.7 x 62.4
Summer Draught	28' 2½" at 12142 dwt.
Built by	Swan, Hunter & Wigham Richardson Ltd.
Year	1962/4
At	Wallsend-on-Tyne
Yard Number	1931
Engine type	Sulzer, 2 stroke, single acting, 6 cylinders.
Speed	16
Built by	Wallsend Slipway Engineers Ltd.
At	Wallsend-on-Tyne
History	Sister to **CLAN FERGUSSON, CLAN FORBES (IV), CLAN FRASER (IV) and CLAN FINLAY.**

1962, January 19: launched for King Line Ltd.

1968: sold to Arya National Shipping Lines Ltd., Iran. Renamed **ARYA SEP.**

1980: transferred on nationalisation to Iran National Shipping Lines. Renamed **IRAN OKHUVAT.**

1983?: sold to Irano-Hind Shipping Co. Ltd. Renamed **OKHUVAT**. The year of this transaction and renaming remains in doubt.

Disposal

1985, September 24: arrived at Mangalore, India, for scrapping.

Photo credit   WSPL

CLAN GRANT (IV)

LR Number	5075012
Official Number	301480
Signal Letters	GHXQ
GRT as built	9322
NRT	5124
Dimensions in feet	loa 496.7 x 62.7
Summer Draught	28' 2¼" at 11870 dwt.
Built by	Greenock Dockyard Co. Ltd.
Year	1962/5
At	Greenock
Yard Number	499
Engine type	Sulzer, 2 stroke, single acting, 6 cylinders.
Speed	16
Built by	Barclay, Curle & Co. Ltd.
At	Whiteinch, Glasgow

History   Sister to **CLAN GRAHAM (IV).**

1962, December 22: launched for Clan Line Steamers Ltd.

1981: sold to Venables Steamship S. A., Panama. Renamed **ENRIQUETA**.

Disposal

1985, January: arrived in China for breaking up.

Photo credit   WSPL

CLAN MACGILLIVRAY (II)

LR Number   5075050
Official Number   304140
Signal Letters   GIGY
GRT as built   9039   **NRT** 4909
Dimensions in feet   loa 507.9 x 63.3
Summer Draught   28' 5¾" at 11930 dwt.
Built by Greenock Dockyard Co. Ltd. **Year** 1962/9 **At** Greenock **Yard Number** 500
Engine type   Sulzer RD76, 2 stroke, single acting, 6 cylinders. **Speed** 16½
Built by   Barclay, Curle & Co. Ltd. **At** Whiteinch, Glasgow
History   This class, the "MAC G's", were fitted with 1 x 60 tons and 2 x 20 tons SWL derricks. This ship's 20 ton derricks were upgraded to 22.5 tons S.W.L.in 1977 for container lifting. She was the first British ship to be built with an air-conditioned control room in the engine-room. Probably my favourite Clan ship. I was Mate on her for over 3 years when she was mainly on the South Africa to Mediterranean trade, due to her having been blacked by the UK dockers for carrying asbestos.
1962, May 22: launched for Clan Line Steamers Ltd.
1969: transferred to King Line Ltd. and back to Clan Line in 1977.
1978, May: called at Piraeus, Greece, and according to the port agent, she was the only Clan Line vessel to call there since the **CLAN FRASER** blew up there in 1941.
1978, June 2: arrived at Venice, then Trieste, Italy, a week later. She was probably the only Clan Line ship to call at those ports.
1981: sold to Gateway Shipping Ltd., Hong Kong, whilst laid up at Chittagong, Bangladesh. Renamed **CLAN MACBOYD.**
Disposal
1984, September 17: departed Singapore for Shanghai, China, where she was broken up.
Photo credit   A.Duncan.

CLAN FINLAY

LR Number	5074977
Official Number	304143
Signal Letters	GJTE
GRT as built	9292
NRT	4993
Dimensions in feet	loa 497.7 x 62.4
Summer Draught	28' 2½" at 11950 dwt.
Built by	Swan, Hunter & Wigham Richardson Ltd.
Year	1962/10
At	Wallsend-on-Tyne
Yard Number	1933
Engine type	Sulzer, 2 stroke, single acting, 6 cylinders.
Speed	16
Built by	Wallsend Slipway.Engineers Ltd.
At	Wallsend-on-Tyne
History	Sister to **CLAN FERGUSSON, CLAN FORBES (IV), CLAN FRASER (IV),** and **CLAN FARQUHARSON**.

1962, June 29: launched for King Line Ltd.

1968: sold to Arya National Shipping Lines, Iran. Renamed **ARYA FAR.**

1971: sold and renamed **ATLANTIC OCEAN** by Tat On Shipping & Enterprises Co. Ltd. of Mogadishu, Somali Republic.

1975: sold to China Ocean Shipping Co, (COSCO), Gusangzhou. Renamed **LU CHUN.**

Disposal

1987 Out of Lloyd's Register of Ships, presumed scrapped.

Photo credit   Real Photo Co.

CLAN MACGREGOR (III)

LR Number	5402643
Official Number	304151
Signal Letters	GKWU
GRT as built	9039
NRT	4909
Dimensions in feet	loa 507.9 x 63.3
Summer Draught	28' 6½" at 12050 dwt.
Built by	Greenock Dockyard Co. Ltd.
Year	1962/12 **At** Greenock **Yard Number** 501
Engine type	Sulzer RD76, 2 stroke, single acting, 6 cylinders. **Speed** 16½
Built by	Barclay, Curle & Co. Ltd. **At** Whiteinch, Glasgow
History	Sister to **CLAN MACGILLIVRAY (II)** and **CLAN MACGOWAN.**

Although these three ships appeared outwardly identical, I can assure readers that there were minor differences when it came to details. The only outward difference that could be seen was that the flag yard attached to the radar mast on each ship was different. I sailed on all three! They were heavily rigged with a very strong weather deck for heavy cargoes.

1962, September 26: launched for King Line Ltd.

1981, November 1: arrived at Avonmouth for discharge before going to Salford, Manchester. She became the last Clan Line ship in service and the last conventional ship to call at Manchester.

1982: sold to Raft Shipping Co., Piraeus, Greece. Renamed **ANGELIKA R.**

Disposal

1982, November 9: she had an engine room fire 60 miles south of Cyprus and was towed to Larnaca Roads. She was declared a constructive total loss.

1983, March 3: arrived at Laurium, Greece, to be broken up.

1983, September: demolition began by G. Perdikarias & Co.

Photo credit   Ken Lowe. Photo in Manchester Ship Canal, November 1981, see above notes.

CLAN MACGOWAN

LR Number	5402631
Official Number	304153
Signal Letters	GKDE
GRT as built	9039
NRT	4909
Dimensions in feet	loa 507.9 x 63.3
Summer Draught	28' 6½" at 12010 dwt.
Built by	Greenock Dockyard Co. Ltd.
Year	1963/4
At	Greenock
Yard Number	502
Engine type	Sulzer RD76, 2 stroke, single acting, 6 cylinders.
Speed	16½
Built by	Wallsend Slipway & Engineering Co. Ltd.
At	Wallsend-on-Tyne
History	Sister to **CLAN MACGILLIVRAY (II)** and **CLAN MACGREGOR (III).**

This ship's engine was built at Wallsend-on-Tyne, unlike those of her sisters, which were Clyde built.

1962, December 14: launched for King Line Ltd.

1970: sold to India S. S. Co. Ltd., Calcutta. Renamed **INDIAN TRIBUNE**.

1979, April 16: sustained serious damage when she was struck by the ro-ro vessel,

BANDAR ABBAS EXPRESS, (O. T. Rederiana, Sweden), whilst berthed at Bombay, India.

Disposal

1984, May 24: laid up at Calcutta, India.

1985, June: demolition commenced by Chaudhary Shipbreaking Co., Calcutta.

Photo credit   A. Blackler & A. Duncan.

CLAN RAMSAY

LR Number	6420410
Official Number	304194
Signal Letters	GMUZ
GRT as built	10542
NRT	5803
Dimensions in feet	loa 529.3 x 68.9
Summer Draught	28' 3¼" at 11730 dwt.
Built by	Greenock Dockyard Co. Ltd.
Year	1965/3
At	Greenock **Yard Number** 506
Engine type	Burmeister & Wain (B&W) 74-VT2BF.160, 2 stroke, single acting, 7 cylinders.
Speed	17½
Built by	J. G. Kincaid & Co. Ltd. **At** Greenock
History	Sister to **CLAN RANALD (V), CLAN ROBERTSON (IV)** and **CLAN ROSS (IV).**

Refrigerated/general cargo vessels not owned by Clan Line Steamers Ltd., but painted in Clan Line livery, until they were renamed in 1977, when they were given the Union-Castle colour scheme.

1964, August 26: launched for Union-Castle Mail S. S. Co. Ltd., (Cayzer Irvine & Co. Ltd., managers).

1977: renamed **WINCHESTER CASTLE**. Union-Castle livery.

1979: placed under the Universal Reefers consortium (U-C / Safmarine).

Renamed **WINCHESTER UNIVERSAL**.

1980: sold to Kappa Maritime Ltd., Greece, but registered under Braganza Bay Shipping Corp., Monrovia,. Renamed **LADY MADONNA**.

Disposal

1985, April 25: arrived Gadani Beach, Pakistan, for breaking up.

Photo credit   M. Lindsay

CLAN ROSS (IV)

LR Number	6522488
Official Number	307645
Signal Letters	GQNE
GRT as built	10541
NRT	5802
Dimensions in feet	loa 529.3 x 68.9
Summer Draught	28' 3" at 11918 dwt.

Built by   Greenock Dockyard Co. Ltd. **Year** 1966/3 **At** Greenock

Yard Number   506. The last ship to be built by this company before it went into liquidation.

Engine type   Burmeister & Wain (B&W) 74-VT2BF.160, 2 stroke, single acting, 7 cylinders.

Speed   17½   **Built by** J. G. Kincaid & Co. Ltd. **At** Greenock

History   Sister to **CLAN RAMSAY, CLAN RANALD (V),**
and **CLAN ROBERTSON (IV)**.

Refrigerated/general cargo vessels not owned by Clan Line Steamers Ltd., but painted in Clan Line livery, until they were renamed in 1977, when they were given the Union-Castle colour scheme.

1965, September 24: launched for Houston Line Ltd., (Cayzer Irvine & Co. Ltd., managers). The last vessel built for that company.

1976, December: transferred to Union-Castle Line. Renamed **KINPURNIE CASTLE (II)**. Changed from Clan Line to Union-Castle livery.

1979: placed under the Universal Reefers consortium (U-C/Safmarine).

Renamed **KINPURNIE UNIVERSAL**; Union-Castle livery.

1982, December: sold to Comninos Bros. (National Heritage Cia. Nav. S. A., manager), Piraeus, Greece. Renamed **SYROS REEFER**. That sale was the end of the Union-Castle Line, at sea.

1984, February 5: grounded in Berkeley Sound, Falkland Islands, during a gale. Later refloated.

Disposal 1984, July 31: arrived at Chittagong, Bangladesh, for breaking up by National Shipbreakers.

Photo credit   M. Lindsay

111

CLAN ALPINE (V)

LR Number	6702557
Official Number	307670
Signal Letters	GTYH
GRT as built	9050
NRT	4900
Dimensions in feet	loa 507.9 x 63.2
Summer Draught	28' 5½" at 12673 dwt
Built by	Scotts' Shipbuilding & Engineering Co. Ltd., (ex Greenock D. Y. Co. Ltd.) at the former Greenock Dockyard site which Scott's had taken over during the building of this vessel.
Year	1967/4
At	Greenock
Yard Number	708
Engine type	Burmeister & Wain (B&W), 2 stroke, single acting, 6 cylinders.
Speed	16
Built by	J. G. Kincaid & Co. Ltd. **At** Greenock
History	Similar to the "CLAN MAC G's".

Appropriately named, as she took the name of the first ship to be built for Clan Line. She was the last ship to be built for Clan Line Steamers Ltd., and the only general cargo one to have mechanical hatch covers. She was fitted with 1 x 60 tons SWL derrick.

1966, December 1: launched for Clan Line Steamers Ltd.

1981: sold to Delibra Shipping Co. Inc., Liberia. Renamed **AFRICAN DIAMOND**.

1982: renamed **PACIFIC AMBER**. Same owners.

Disposal

1984, May 2: arrived at Kaohsiung, Taiwan, for breaking up

Photo credit   WSPL + Anon

KING ALFRED

Ex Names	**ANGELUS** - Launched as **HEMSEFJELL** - 1968 fitted out as
LR Number	6812857
Official Number	335920 (registered at London)
Signal Letters	GYVG - Telex No. 45985 (a sign of modern communications!)
GRT as built	29119
NRT	22134
Dimensions in feet	loa 713.9 x 97.2
Summer Draught	42' 00½" at 54250 dwt.

Built by Eriksbergs, M/V A/B   **Year** 1968/9 **At** Göthenburg, Sweden   **Yard Number**   616

Engine type   Burmeister & Wain (B&W), 8-74VT2BF160, 2 stroke, single acting, 8 cylinders.

Speed   16   **Built by** Eriksbergs M/V A/B   **At**   Göthenburg, Sweden

History

She is a bulk carrier with 7 holds, strengthened for ore cargo.

1968, April 2: launched as **ANGELUS** for H. Angel Olsen, Norway. Sold whilst fitting out to Olsen & Ugelstad, Oslo, Norway. Renamed **HEMSEFJELL**.

1968, September: delivered from the builders to King Line Ltd., as **KING ALFRED.**

1977: transferred to Houston Line but painted in Clan Line colours.

1980, February: transferred to Clan Line Ltd. King Line livery.

1982: transferred to Cayzer Irvine & Co. Ltd., but still in King Line livery.

1983: sold to China Ocean Shipping Co. (COSCO), Guanzhou, China.
Renamed **LUO FU SHAN.**

Disposal

2002: still in Lloyd's Register of Ships. The owner is given as China Shipping International Intermodal Co. Ltd., Guangzhou, China. She is the last remaining ship to have carried the famous 2 red bands on black.

Photo credit   Anon + A. J. Blackler

114

KING JAMES

Ex Name	**ARALAR** - launched as
LR Number	7011591
Official Number	339322 (registered at London)
Signal Letters	GOOL
GRT as built	30289
NRT	20462
Dimensions in feet	loa 678.9 x 95.3
Summer Draught	43' 7" at 52558 dwt.

Built by   Astilleros Españoles S. A.   **Year**   1970/10

At   Matagorda, Cadiz, Spain   **Yard Number** 158

Engine type   Sulzer 6RNDS90, 2 stroke, single acting, 6 cylinders.   **Speed**   15¼

Built by   Astilleros Españoles S. A.   **At**   Sestao, Spain

History   Sister to **KING CHARLES (II)**.

She was a bulk carrier with 7 holds, strengthened for ore cargo. Registered under King Line Ltd., but wore Clan Line livery, as did most King Line owned or named ships after the merger in 1956.

1970, February 21: launched for Naviera Artola, Spain, as **ARALAR**. Purchased by British & Commonwealth Group while fitting out. Registered in the ownership of King Line Ltd.

1970: October: completed as **KING JAMES.**

1978: Sold to Gwarnek & Co., Liberia. Renamed **NUMBER FOUR**.

1980, May 28: suffered extensive fire damage to her accommodation off Bombay, India.

1982: renamed **TYNE** by her owners, presumably for her final voyage to the breakers.

Disposal

1982: sold to Italian shipbreakers at Spezia.

1982, September 24: arrived at Spezia prior to this date and was broken up by Cantieri di Santa Maria.

Photo credit   M. Lindsay

KING CHARLES (II)

LR Number	7363437
Official Number	363376 (registered at London)
Signal Letters	GTUT
GRT as built	30276
NRT	20454
Dimensions in feet	loa 678.3 x 95.3
Summer Draught	43' 7" at 54256 dwt.
Built by	Astilleros Españoles S. A.
Year	1974/7
At	Matagorda, Cadiz, Spain
Yard Number	176
Engine type	Sulzer 6RNDS90, 2 stroke, single acting, 6 cylinders.
Speed	15¼
Built by	Astilleros Españoles S. A.
At	Bilbao, Spain
History	Bulk carrier. Sister to **KING JAMES.**

1973, December: launched for King Line Ltd.

1982: transferred to the ownership of Cayzer Irvine & Co. Ltd. Same name.

1983: sold by King Line to ILC Marine Corp. Ltd., Liberia. Renamed **CYPRESS.**

1988: sold to Aquafaith Shipping, Cyprus. Renamed **ALFA.**

1988, November 16: collided with the bulk carrier **SEADRIVE** in the Langelands Belt, Denmark. The collision caused extensive damage aft.

Disposal

1996, July 30: arrived at Alang, India, for breaking up.

1996, August 8: demolition commenced by International Steel Corp., Alang, India.

Photo credit   Blackler collection (Anon)

SCOTTISH EAGLE (II)

LR Number	7391939
Official Number	388314
Signal Letters	GBJM
GRT as built	32995
NRT	21625
Dimensions in feet	loa 689.0 x 105.9
Summer Draught	40' 6 $^3/_8$" at 59645 dwt.

Built by   Cammell Laird Shipbuilders Ltd.

Year   1980/3

At   Birkenhead

Yard Number   1373

Engine type   Sulzer 6RND90, 2 stroke, single acting, 6 cylinders.

Speed   15

Built by   G. Clark & North East Marine Ltd. **At** Wallsend-on-Tyne

History   Sister to **SCOTTISH LION (II).**

1979: July 13: launched for King Line Ltd., but operated by Scottish Tankers Ltd. Scottish Tankers livery. Not strictly a Clan Line vessel.

1982: One of a number of ships taken up from trade (STUFT) by the Ministry of Defence for duties in the Falkland Islands during the conflict there. She was based in San Carlos Water.

1986: sold to Seaplace Shipping Ltd., Cyprus. Renamed **SEAMAGIC**. Her sale ended the shipping business of the Cayzer family. The last vestiges of Clan Line and its associated shipping companies, except for artefacts and memories, went with her.

1989: sold to Guangzhou Maritime Transport (Group) Co. Ltd., China. Renamed **GUI HE.**

Disposal

2003: still in service.

Photo credit   T. Bolton.

INDEX

INDEX

INDEX

INDEX

INDEX

Note: Bold Type equals Clan Line ships with full details.

Possible erratta.

Vol 1 p7. It is possible that the photograph is not the Clan Menzies. It is likely to be the Clan Maclaren (I) or Clan MacFadyen (I).

Vol 2 Pgs 71 & 72 The photographs of the Clan Cumming (II) and the Clan Buchanan (II) are not those that go with the text. Both ships were wartime losses and the photographs shown are their replacements. The differences are very slight and to most people almost indistinguishable.

My apologies but I was guided by the names and dates written on the the back of all the photographs

AJB 2003

For your own notes.

MORE GREAT BOOKS AND VIDEOS FROM AVID

THETIS -THE ADMIRALTY REGRETS -The Disaster in Liverpool Bay
by C.Warren & J.Benson

The definitive minute by minute account of this terrible tragedy in 1939 when 99 souls lost their lives as HM Submarine *Thetis* undertook her first and only dive. With new photographs and documents as well as a new foreword by Derek Arnold, a survivors son, and a new postscript by maritime historian David Roberts. Why didn't anyone cut open the submarine? Why was there no urgency in the Admiralty's rescue system?

Did the Admiralty really regret?

ISBN 0 9521020 8 0   £12.00 inc. p&p

HMS THETIS - SECRETS AND SCANDAL
by David Roberts

This book uncovers some shocking hitherto unpublished details of the events and aftermath of this terrible Submarine disaster in1939. Why did the Official Inquiry blame nobody, explaining it away as 'an unfortunate sequence of events'? Why did the civil action on behalf of the widows fail?

Did the Admiralty cover it up? How much did Churchill know?
How were those left behind treated?

ISBN 0 9521020 0 5   £11.50 inc. p&p

132

THE ALABAMA AFFAIR
- THE BRITISH SHIPYARDS CONSPIRACY IN THE AMERICAN CIVIL WAR
by David Hollett

This book reveals the turmoil and intrigue surrounding a deal involving the British government, the now defunct Merseyside shipyard of Cammell Laird and a country engaged in civil war, America.

· *What was involved?* · *How was the conspiracy organised?*
· *Who were the shadowy figures at the centre of the controversy?*

The *Alabama* Affair answers all the questions.

ISBN 1 902964 32 2   £12.50 inc. p&p

BLUE FUNNEL - VOYAGE EAST
by Award Winning author RICHARD WOODMAN

'This is life at sea, warts and all, and a better book because of it.' Sea Breezes

A new and revised version of this classic tale of a typical Blue Funnel Cargo Liner in the middle of the 20th century.
Contains new photographs of many of the 'Blue Flue' vessels.
'The work of a practised writer...a deeply felt...account of merchant shipping in the 1960s...shrewd and readable...' Sunday Times

ISBN 1 902964 0 4 7   £12.50 inc. p&p

LUSITANIA

by Colin Simpson

More than eighty years on the story of the *Lusitania* continues to be shrouded in mystery and suspicion. What was her real cargo? Why wasn't she protected? Why did she sink so quickly?
The Facts, the fictions, but most of all...the truth.

'A book that clamours to be read...' - The Observer
ISBN 0 9521020 6 4
£12.50 inc. p&p

FORGOTTEN EMPRESS - THE TRAGEDY OF THE EMPRESS OF IRELAND
By David Zeni

'...dubbed 'The 'Forgotten Empress'...the second in a shocking trio of tragedies at sea...sandwiched in between the disasters of the Titanic *and the* Lusitania, *...it was a sudden death... that sent Liverpool into mourning...'* Liverpool Echo

ISBN 1 902964 15 2
£12.50 inc. p&p

THE GOLDEN WRECK - THE LOSS OF THE *ROYAL CHARTER*
By Alexander McKee

The effects great of the great hurricane of October 1859 were to shock the nation. 133 ships were sunk, 90 were badly damaged and almost 800 people lost their lives.

More than half of those that perished were on one ship - *The Royal Charter*.

The worst shipwreck in Welsh history, this is the story of the *Royal Charter*...and her gold.

ISBN 1 902964 0 2 0 £12.00 inc. p&p

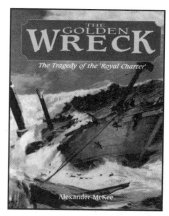

IRON CLIPPER '*TAYLEUR*' – the White Star Line's 'First Titanic'
by H.F. Starkey

'Iron Clipper' is subtitled 'The First Titanic' for it tells the story of the first White Star liner to be lost on her maiden voyage. The *'Tayleur'* tragedy of 1854 and the '*Titanic'* catastrophe of 1912 are disasters which have so much in common that the many coincidences make this book appear to be a work which is stranger than fiction.

ISBN 1 902964 00 4

£9.00 inc. p&p

LIFE AT LAIRDS - MEMORIES OF WORKING SHIPYARD MEN
by David Roberts

When Cammell Lairds has gone and we are a generation or two down the line who will answer the questions 'What did they do there?' 'What was it like?' This book answers the questions.

- Sea Breezes

A Piece of Social History – Liverpool Echo

ISBN 0 9521020 1 3

£ 8.50 inc. p&p

{Cammell Laird - Old ships and Hardships: on Video. £15.95 inc. p&p in UK}

CAMMELL LAIRD - THE GOLDEN YEARS
by David Roberts.
Foreword by Frank Field MP

'Captures life in the prosperous years of the historic Birkenhead shipyard'- Liverpool Echo

'Puts into perspective...the strikes...the Polaris contract...and those who worked at the yard'

- Sea Breezes

ISBN 0 9521020 2 1

£7.95   inc. p&p

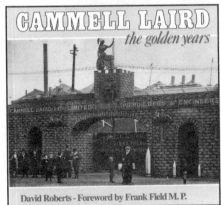

LUSITANIA AND BEYOND - the Life of Captain William Thomas Turner
by Mitch Peeke and Kevin Walsh Johnson
Over the years Captain Turner has been accused of treachery, stubbornness, ignorance and much worse. This book gives the true, remarkable story of Captain William Thomas Turner, the last Master of the doomed *Lusitania*.
ISBN   1 902964 14 4   £9.50 inc. p&p

A WELCOME IN THE HILLSIDES ? - The Merseyside and North Wales Experience of Evacuation by Jill Wallis
A book that is both informative and moving, with the real-life stories of the thousands of children who left the dangers of Merseyside for the safety of North Wales during World War II.
ISBN   1 902964 13 6   £12.50 inc. p&p

THE LIVERPOOL LIFEBOAT DISASTER OF 1892- One man's search for a missing piece of history - by Jim Sullivan
'A labour of love that deserves to be told... a story of astonishing courage, brilliantly researched.' - Alan Bleasdale   ISBN   1 902964 10 1 £9.00 inc. p&p

JUST NUISANCE AB - His Full Story by Terence Sisson
The amazing but true story of the only dog that was officially enlisted into the British Royal Navy, a Great Dane whose name was Nuisance, his official rank and name was AB Just Nuisance. Famed for his preference for the company of navy ratings (he wasn't too keen on Officers) in and around the famous World War II naval base of Simonstown, South Africa, Nuisance helped many a sailor rejoin his ship after a night on the town.   £10.00 inc. p&p

FROM BATTLEFIELD TO BLIGHTY

A History of Frodsham Auxiliary Hospital 1915-1919

by Arthur R Smith

The horrors of the first 'Great War' are well known, but the stories of those sent back from the 'Battlefield to Blighty' tend to be overlooked. This is the little known story in words and photographs of one of the largest auxiliary military hospitals in the country that was established at Frodsham in Cheshire during the First World War.

ISBN 1 9029640 16 0   £8.50 inc. p&p

FASTER THAN THE WIND - A History Guide to the Liverpool to Holyhead Telegraph.

by Frank Large

Take a journey along the one of most spectacular coastlines in Britain, the hills and countryside of North Wales and Wirral. The views are quite superb, and on a clear day it is possible to see just how signals about shipping were sent along the coast to and from Liverpool. This book contains full details of the intriguing and little known sites of the substantial remains of the Liverpool to Holyhead Telegraph Stations.

£11.00 inc. p&p

THE FIRST TWO VOLUMES IN THE CLAN LINE IN PHOTOGRAPHS SERIES

VOL I - THE FIRST 40 YEARS 1878 -1918
VOL II - FROM PEACE TO PEACE 1918-1945

£10.00 inc. p&p each volume

V I D E O S

BLUE FUNNEL - VOYAGES AND VOICES

Vittoria dock in Birkenhead was the home of what was once the biggest and probably the best General Cargo shipping company in Britain; Alfred Holt's... perhaps better known as 'The Blue Funnel Line' or ' the 'China Boats'. Many thousands of people, both passengers and crews sailed on famous ships like 'Hector' 'Patroclus', 'Laomedon' and many more.

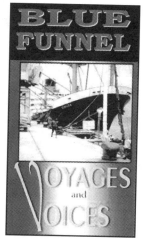

This new video has been compiled with the help of never before published film taken all over the world by some of those men who actually sailed with 'Blueys' on many of their well-known vessels.

Contains some of the sights and sounds of typical Blue Funnel voyages; leaving the home shores of the UK, sailing through both the Suez and Panama canals, the legendary gilly gilly man, Hong Kong, Singapore, Kobe, Tokyo, and other 'exotic' ports.

We also see and hear the thoughts and memories of some of those who actually sailed with 'Blueys' over their working lives, from Able Seaman to Captain, Steward to Engineer.

The film is a must for anyone who sailed with 'Blueys' or who sailed in the merchant navy of old.

Running time approx: 55.00 mins. £15.95 inc. Post and Packaging in UK.

CAMMELL LAIRD - OLD SHIPS AND HARDSHIPS - THE STORY OF A SHIPYARD.

After an extensive search for moving footage of this world famous shipyard at work, a video of the history of the yard has at last been compiled. How Cammell Laird served the nation through two World Wars, building world famous vessels like the *Rodney, Hood, Mauritania, Ark Royal, Windsor Castle* and many more, up to the tragic day in 1993 when Lairds was shut down. The story of the yard is also told through the voices of the men who worked at Lairds; Welders, Cranedrivers, Electricians and Plumbers, they tell of the hardships of building ships in all weathers and the lighter moments that came from some of the 'characters' of the shipyard.

Running time approx: 55.00 mins. £15.95 inc. Post and Packaging in UK.

{ Overseas formats are available on request }

ALL IN A DAY'S WORK - VOLUME I & VOLUME II
- *LOOKING AT ORDINARY WORKING LIVES ON THE RIVER MERSEY.*

£15.95 inc. Post and Packaging in UK. { Overseas formats are available on request }

To Order Books and Videos Direct Contact:-

Avid Publications, Garth Boulevard, Hr. Bebington, Wirral, Merseyside UK. CH63 5LS.

Tel / Fax (44) 0151 645 2047

Look at the books and videos via the internet on

http://www.avidpublications.co.uk or e-mail info@avidpublications.co.uk

Note. All prices include postage and packaging within UK.